Lecture Notes in Computer Science　　　10220

Commenced Publication in 1973
Founding and Former Series Editors:
Gerhard Goos, Juris Hartmanis, and Jan van Leeuwen

More information about this series at http://www.springer.com/series/8183

Marina L. Gavrilova · C.J. Kenneth Tan (Eds.)

Transactions on Computational Science XXIX

 Springer

Editors-in-Chief

Marina L. Gavrilova
University of Calgary
Calgary, AB
Canada

C.J. Kenneth Tan
Sardina Systems
Tallinn
Estonia

ISSN 0302-9743 ISSN 1611-3349 (electronic)
Lecture Notes in Computer Science
ISSN 1866-4733 ISSN 1866-4741 (electronic)
Transactions on Computational Science
ISBN 978-3-662-54562-1 ISBN 978-3-662-54563-8 (eBook)
DOI 10.1007/978-3-662-54563-8

Library of Congress Control Number: 2017935025

Printed on acid-free paper

This Springer imprint is published by Springer Nature
The registered company is Springer-Verlag GmbH Germany
The registered company address is: Heidelberger Platz 3, 14197 Berlin, Germany

LNCS Transactions on Computational Science

Computational science, an emerging and increasingly vital field, is now widely recognized as an integral part of scientific and technical investigations, affecting researchers and practitioners in areas ranging from aerospace and automotive research to biochemistry, electronics, geosciences, mathematics, and physics. Computer systems research and the exploitation of applied research naturally complement each other. The increased complexity of many challenges in computational science demands the use of supercomputing, parallel processing, sophisticated algorithms, and advanced system software and architecture. It is therefore invaluable to have input by systems research experts in applied computational science research.

Transactions on Computational Science focuses on original high-quality research in the realm of computational science in parallel and distributed environments, also encompassing the underlying theoretical foundations and the applications of large-scale computation.

The journal offers practitioners and researchers the opportunity to share computational techniques and solutions in this area, to identify new issues, and to shape future directions for research, and it enables industrial users to apply leading-edge, large-scale, high-performance computational methods.

In addition to addressing various research and application issues, the journal aims to present material that is validated – crucial to the application and advancement of the research conducted in academic and industrial settings. In this spirit, the journal focuses on publications that present results and computational techniques that are verifiable.

Scope

The scope of the journal includes, but is not limited to, the following computational methods and applications:

- Aeronautics and Aerospace
- Astrophysics
- Big Data Analytics
- Bioinformatics
- Biometric Technologies
- Climate and Weather Modeling
- Communication and Data Networks
- Compilers and Operating Systems
- Computer Graphics
- Computational Biology
- Computational Chemistry
- Computational Finance and Econometrics

- Computational Fluid Dynamics
- Computational Geometry
- Computational Number Theory
- Data Representation and Storage
- Data Mining and Data Warehousing
- Information and Online Security
- Grid Computing
- Hardware/Software Co-design
- High-Performance Computing
- Image and Video Processing
- Information Systems
- Information Retrieval
- Modeling and Simulations
- Mobile Computing
- Numerical and Scientific Computing
- Parallel and Distributed Computing
- Robotics and Navigation
- Supercomputing
- System-on-Chip Design and Engineering
- Virtual Reality and Cyberworlds
- Visualization

Editorial

The Transactions on Computational Science journal is part of the Springer series *Lecture Notes in Computer Science*, and is devoted to a range of computational science issues, from theoretical aspects to application-dependent studies and the validation of emerging technologies.

The journal focuses on original high-quality research in the realm of computational science in parallel and distributed environments, encompassing the theoretical foundations and the applications of large-scale computations and massive data processing. Practitioners and researchers share computational techniques and solutions in the area, identify new issues, and shape future directions for research, as well as enable industrial users to apply the techniques presented.

The current volume is devoted to the topic of secure and reliable communications, as well as signal and image processing. It is comprised of seven full papers, presenting algorithms for secure communication, including recovering weak radio signals, designing efficient circuits, providing multiple antenna sensing techniques, examining the relationship between modes of intercomputer communications and fault types, discovering new ways to efficiently and reliably build geometric meshes, and studying big data processing in distributed environments.

We would like to extend our sincere appreciation to all the reviewers for their work on this regular issue. Our special thanks go to Editorial Assistant Ms. Madeena Sultana, for her dedicated work on collecting papers and communicating with authors. We would also like to thank all of the authors for submitting their papers to the journal and the associate editors and referees for their valuable work.

It is our hope that this collection of eight articles presented in this issue will be a valuable resource for Transactions on Computational Science readers and will stimulate further research into the key area of high-performance computing.

January 2017

Marina L. Gavrilova
C.J. Kenneth Tan

LNCS Transactions on Computational Science – Editorial Board

Contents

Analysis of Relationship Between Modes of Intercomputer Communications and Fault Types in Redundant Computer Systems

Refik Samet[1(✉)] and Nermin Samet[2]

[1] Ankara University, Ankara, Turkey
samet@eng.ankara.edu.tr
[2] Middle East Technical University, Ankara, Turkey
nermin.samet@gmail.com

Abstract. This paper analyzes the reasons of appearance of non‑Byzantine and Byzantine fault types in redundant computer systems. The proposed approach is based on analysis of the relationship between the modes of intercomputer communications and fault types. This analysis allows the users to design the redundant computer systems in such a way that Byzantine faults cannot appear. Consequently, designing the redundant computer systems, in which Byzantine faults cannot appear, allows the designers to increase the degree of reliability by preventing the masking of any forms of appearance of faults and by decreasing the time period of checkpoints. In addition, this approach decreases the cost of software and hardware involved in the execution of fault-tolerant procedures.

Keywords: Reliability · Fault-tolerance · Redundant computer system · Non-Byzantine and Byzantine fault types · Byzantine agreement algorithm · Protocols of intercomputer communications · Modes of intercomputer communications

1 Introduction

A control system can be viewed as a combination of two interdependent components: the controlled process and the controlling computer. Detailed analysis of the reliability of real-time control systems is required due to their increasing amount of critical applications; e.g. aircraft, spacecraft, nuclear reactor control, etc., where a failure in the controlling computer would result in catastrophic losses. The reliability of a system is a function of time, $R(t)$, defined as a conditional probability that the system performs correctly throughout the interval of time, $[t_0, t_1]$, given that the system was performing correctly at time t_0 [1,2]. In applications such as those mentioned above the probability of working correctly throughout that interval must be equal to or greater than 0.9999999 "7 nines") [2–5].

© Springer-Verlag GmbH Germany 2017
M.L. Gavrilova and C.J. Kenneth Tan (Eds.): Trans. on Comput. Sci. XXIX, LNCS 10220, pp. 1–32, 2017.
DOI: 10.1007/978-3-662-54563-8_1

"7 nines" is too difficult to reach by using classical methods. Achieving that degree requires a more comprehensive approach including careful optimization of checkpoint time period and preventing the masking of appearance of any fault forms.

Reliable computer system (controlling computer) must handle malfunctioning components that give conflicting information to different parts of the system. In literature, such behavior is denoted as a Byzantine fault. The problem of coping with this type of faults is expressed abstractly as the Byzantine Generals Problem [6–13]. In [7], several solutions to the Byzantine Generals Problem were presented and it has been shown that these solutions are expensive in both the amount of time and number of message required.

There are many fault-tolerant architectures tolerating Byzantine faults, such as MAFT [14], GUARDS [15,16], SIFT [17], FTMP [18]. In these systems, the computational overhead of maintaining fault-tolerance due to Byzantine faults consumes a considerable part of the system throughput. For example, this value is 80% of the system throughput for SIFT and 60% for FTMP.

Recently, researchers have proposed some protocols and algorithms which reduce Byzantine agreement overhead in distributed systems, computer networks, wireless sensor networks, mobile ad hoc networks [19–34]. For example, according to a protocol proposed in [22], each computer in distributed systems can agree on a common value through three rounds of message exchange. Agreement protocol proposed in [23] helps in achieving faster execution results using an effective view change mechanism in distributed computing systems. Protocol proposed in [24] reaches a common agreement within the mobile ad hoc networks by using the minimum number of rounds of message exchange and tolerates a maximum number of allowable faulty components. Byzantine consensus protocol presented in [25] tolerates dynamic message omissions and allows an efficient utilization of the wireless broadcasting medium in wireless ad hoc networks. In [26], authors present two Byzantine fault-tolerant algorithms, which require only $(2k + 1)$ round of message exchange, instead of the usual $(3k + 1)$. Protocol named Zyzzyva [27] reduces replication overheads to near their theoretical minima and achieves throughputs of tens of thousands of requests per second, making Byzantine Fault Tolerance replication practical for a broad range of demanding services. Furthermore, since 2008, new technologies such as OpenMP and CUDA are widely used for fault tolerance [35–44].

Two fault types are recognized in Redundant Computer Systems (RCS): non-Byzantine and Byzantine [1,7,45–49]. The Byzantine fault type has some important problems which cause a checkpoint time period to be increased and some forms of appearance of faults to be masked [7,47]. A key question concerns the reasons for the appearance of Byzantine fault type. Why does a Byzantine fault appear in RCS? Is it possible to design RCS in which Byzantine faults cannot appear?

In [7], the authors explain that due to a marginal signal "hardware" solutions do not solve the Byzantine fault problem. Certainly, a marginal signal is a serious problem in networks and distributed systems [50,51].

However the subject of this study is RCS which consist of the same special computers placed close to each other, often on the same card. We assume that transmitted signals cannot weaken to a marginal level in RCS. We also assume that broadcasting data over a single wire removes the possibility of appearance of Byzantine fault types in RCS. So we do not analyze the non-Byzantine and Byzantine fault types which arise from marginal logic.

We analyze the non-Byzantine and Byzantine fault types which arise from faulty states of the units (input unit, central processing unit and output unit) in RCS. We analyze different intercomputer communication protocols and suggest ones which allow the designers to build RCS that are free from Byzantine fault type.

Broadcast mode is also used in MAFT [14], GUARDS [15] and SIFT [17]. In these architectures, the motivation for choosing this mode is not that it avoids Byzantine behavior. As we will show in Sect. 4, it is possible to design different protocols by using broadcast and other modes of intercomputer communications. Some protocols using broadcast mode avoid Byzantine behavior and others do not. The protocols used in [14,15,17] cannot avoid Byzantine faults.

The main aims of this paper are: (1) to analyze the problems related to Byzantine fault type; (2) to define the reasons of appearance of non-Byzantine and Byzantine fault types by analyzing the relationship between the modes of intercomputer communications and fault types; (3) to suggest rules for building RCS in which Byzantine faults cannot appear.

This paper is organized as follows: in Sect. 2, we describe models which are used in this paper; in Sect. 3, we analyze the problems of Byzantine fault types; in Sect. 4 we analyze the modes of intercomputer communications and protocols in RCS; Sect. 5 analyses the relationship between the modes of intercomputer communications and fault types in RCS; Sect. 6 gives the evaluation and results; the conclusions are made in Sect. 7.

2 Models

2.1 System Model

We consider systems which consist of redundant computers (nodes) (Fig. 1). The typical structure of RCS consists of the same special computers placed close to each other, often on the same card. Redundant computers are connected directly and exchange by data using protocols of intercomputer communications [52–61]. Level of redundancy (the number of redundant nodes) depends on the required degree of reliability. RCS may be formed of double, triple, ..., N - modular redundant nodes [2,3,45,49,57,62–64]. The redundant nodes perform the same single instruction stream on the basis of the same single data stream. The environment of RCS is the redundant sensors and executive devices. We don't investigate RCS based on computers of networks and distributed systems.

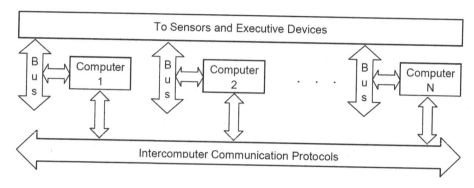

Fig. 1. The typical structure of RCS

2.2   Fault Models

In RCS, we distinguish a non-Byzantine fault type from a Byzantine one according to their effects. Non-Byzantine fault type causes the faulty node to send the same value to all normally operating nodes. On the other hand, Byzantine fault type causes the faulty node to send different values to all normally operating nodes (Example 1 in Appendix I).

We consider two sorts of each fault type. Each fault type may occur either due to transient faults or due to permanent faults [1–3,15,49,61,64–68]. A transient fault is an instantaneous destruction of the logical series for task execution. For example, splashes in output voltage may result in a transient fault. A permanent fault is a permanent destruction of the logical series for task execution. For example, short circuited computer components may result in a permanent fault. Intermittent, semi permanent and other faults may be interpreted either as transient or permanent faults, depending on the time in which they occur. If any fault continues its effects, for example, for more than three sequential logical segments, it may be interpreted as a permanent fault, instead of transient fault. The number of segments to interpret the sort of the fault may be changed from application to application [47].

We investigate special purpose systems where only hardware faults can occur, the probability of appearance of the software bugs is negligible. Malicious attacks cannot occur in systems isolated from general purpose networks or Internet.

2.3   Computational Process Model

Figure 2 shows the typical structure of a computational process that is executed in each node of RCS simultaneously and consists of a number of operating cycles. Each operating cycle consists of M logical segments in which a certain number of real-time application tasks is executed. After each logical segment, the checkpoint is realized [4,69,70]. In a checkpoint, the fault-tolerant procedure is executed. The computational process is formed by serial execution of logical segments and checkpoints. The computational result of the logical segment is represented by a single value (for example, checksum). In the checkpoints, all nodes realize the interchange by computational results. Every node forms the Initial Data Set (IDS) consisting of N elements. IDS are used for execution of the fault-tolerant procedure.

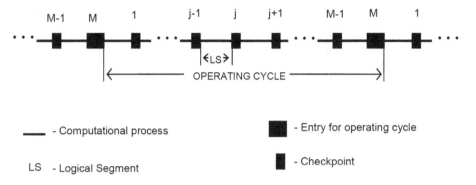

Fig. 2. The typical structure of computational process

The fault-tolerant procedure is a sequence of operations executed by each node to detect and counteract faults. Each complete part of the fault-tolerant procedure is a step which executes certain functions to detect and counteract the faults. Types and steps of the fault-tolerant procedure are listed in Table 1.

As seen from Table 1, there are two types of fault-tolerant procedure. Type 1 is oriented to detect and counteract only non-Byzantine fault type in RCS and consists of five steps. However Type 2 is oriented to detect and counteract both Byzantine and non-Byzantine fault types in RCS and consists of six steps. Consequently Type 2 requires more time and provides higher reliability.

2.4   Basic Assumptions and Limitations

1. We assume that only a single fault may appear during any single logical segment and single checkpoint together.
2. We consider RCS which degrade from N to 1. After any permanent fault the faulty node is closed and RCS continues the computational process with a reduced number of nodes.
3. We also assume that the wired medium (connections) between nodes is fault free. This basically assumes away the possibility of a faulty transmitter transmitting a marginal logic level that is interpreted differently by different receivers. Under this assumption, different receivers interpret a signal on a bus in the same way.

2.5   Main Contributions

The paper aims at providing design rules for building RCS that are free from Byzantine faults. To this end, this paper makes the following contributions:

Table 1. Types and steps of fault-tolerant procedures to detect and counteract the faults in RCS

Step number	Steps of the fault-tolerant procedure	Types of the fault-tolerant procedure			
		Type 1: Fault-tolerant procedure for detecting and counteracting of only non-Byzantine fault type in RCS		Type 2: Fault-tolerant procedure for detecting and counteracting of both Byzantine and non-Byzantine fault types in RCS	
		Steps belonging to the procedure of Type 1	Time period for execution of the appropriate steps	Steps belonging to the procedure of Type 2	Time period for execution of the appropriate steps
1	Execution of the Byzantine agreement algorithm	-	-	✓	t_1
2	Detection of the fault	✓	t_2	✓	t_2
3	Localization of fault (definition of a number of faulty node)	✓	t_3	✓	t_3
4	Definition of the sort of the fault (transient or permanent)	✓	t_4	✓	t_4
5	Recovery of computational process after transient fault	✓	t_5	✓	t_5
6	Reconfiguration of RCS after permanent fault	✓	t_6	✓	t_6

1. This paper defines and analyzes the problems related to Byzantine fault type.
2. This paper also analyzes four modes of intercomputer communications, describes seven protocols by using these modes and gives examples for implementation of these protocols.
3. This paper analyzes the relationship between the modes of intercomputer communications (such as the broadcast, time sharing, non-regular and regular modes) and fault types (such as non-Byzantine and Byzantine) in RCS.
4. This paper defines the reasons for appearance of non-Byzantine and Byzantine fault types on the basis of the regular features of fault types in RCS.
5. This paper shows how the Byzantine fault type affects the degrees of reliability and performance of RCS.

3 An Analysis of Problems Related to Byzantine Fault Type

3.1 Possibilities of RCS to Counteract the Fault Types

Let N be the total number of nodes, k - the number of faulty nodes or the number of faults appeared in RCS and m - the number of communication rounds between

Table 2. Fault types and possibilities of RCS to counteract faults

Number of nodes in RCS	Fault types	Possibilities of RCS to counteract the fault types
1	Special case: A system is not redundant	
2	Only non-Byzantine fault type can appear	Only non-Byzantine fault type can be counteracted
3	Both non-Byzantine and Byzantine fault types can appear	It is possible to counteract only non-Byzantine fault type because there are no mechanisms to counteract the Byzantine fault type in RCS with $N = 3$
From 4 to N	Both non-Byzantine and Byzantine fault types can appear	Both non-Byzantine and Byzantine fault types can be counteracted

nodes for execution of a fault-tolerant procedure. Table 2 presents the fault types and possibilities of RCS to counteract them.

Table 3 shows the relationship between N, k, m and fault types which can be counteracted in RCS.

In order to counteract the Byzantine fault type, several algorithms have been proposed to solve the Byzantine agreement problem: (1) Determinate, (2) Approximate and (3) Randomize [7, 46, 71–74]. These algorithms require all non-faulty nodes to agree on an identical value. All that these algorithms can do is guarantee that all computers use the same input value [7]. In other words, these

Table 3. Relationship between N, k, m and fault types

Number of faults (k)	A single fault may appear during any single logical segment and single checkpoint together[a]				k faults may appear during any single logical segment and single checkpoint together[b]			
	Required number (N) of nodes for counteracting		Required number (m) of communication rounds for counteracting		Required number (N) of nodes for counteracting		Required number (m) of communication rounds for counteracting	
	non-Byzantine fault type	Byzantine fault type	non-Byzantine fault type	Byzantine fault type	non-Byzantine fault type	Byzantine fault type	non-Byzantine fault type	Byzantine fault type
1	2	4	1	2	3	4	1	2
2	3	5	1	2	5	7	1	3
...	...	...	...	...	...	...	...	...
k	$N \geq k+1$	$N \geq k+3$	$m = 1$	$m = 2$	$N \geq 2k+1$	$N \geq 3k+1$	$m = 1$	$m = k+1$

[a] After permanent fault, faulty node is closed, RCS is degraded and the computational process is continued with reduced number of non-faulty nodes.
[b] After permanent fault, faulty node is not closed, RCS continues the computational process with the same number of nodes but part of them is faulty.

algorithms reduce almost all forms of appearance of faults to the same form as for a non-Byzantine fault type. In this paper, we will use the Determinate Byzantine agreement algorithm for describing the forms of appearance of faults.

Two sequential actions are realized for detecting and counteracting of the Byzantine fault type: (1) conversion of the Byzantine fault type to the non-Byzantine fault type by using the Byzantine agreement algorithms and (2) counteracting of the fault by using the fault-tolerant procedure oriented for non-Byzantine fault type.

3.2   Problems Related to Byzantine Fault Type

Problem #1: Masking of some forms of appearance of faults is a serious problem. During execution of Byzantine agreement algorithm, the value of each element of final IDS is generated by majority voting, i.e., it is equal to the value of the majority of agreements [7,14,15,17,46,47]. As a result, the majority voting procedure hides the forms of appearance of faults for which the number of disagreements is less than one half of the total number of elements in a group and these forms of appearance of faults may build up and ultimately lead to system failure (Cases 2.1, 2.2, and 2.3 of Example 2 in Appendix I).

Problem #2: It is impossible to counteract the Byzantine fault type appearing in RCS with $N = 3$ [7,46,47]. It is known that there is only one way to counteract the Byzantine fault type, which is by using the Byzantine agreement protocols. However, these protocols are used only for RCS where ($N \geq 3k+1$) (Example 3 in Appendix I). Therefore, the Byzantine fault type directly decreases the degree of reliability of RCS with $N = 3$.

Problem #3: The Byzantine fault type requires more software, hardware and processing time [7,14,15,17,47].

(a) The fault-tolerant procedure for non-Byzantine fault type consists of five steps, whereas for Byzantine fault type, it consists of six steps. The first step is for conversion of Byzantine fault type to non-Byzantine type by using Byzantine agreement protocols and the other five steps are the same as with the fault-tolerant procedure for a non-Byzantine fault (Table 1). So, software for realization of the fault-tolerant procedure for the Byzantine fault type includes 6 steps instead of the 5 steps for non-Byzantine one.

(b) In order to counteract k Byzantine faults ($N \geq k+3$)[a] (or ($N \geq 3k+1$)[b]) nodes are required instead of ($N \geq k+1$)[a] (or ($N \geq 2k+1$)[b]) node for k non-Byzantine faults (for a and b see notes under Table 3). For example, for counteracting $k = 2$ Byzantine faults, minimum ($N \geq 5$)[a] (or ($N \geq 7$)[b]) nodes and for counteracting of the same number of non-Byzantine faults, minimum ($N \geq 3$)[a] (or ($N \geq 5$)[b]) nodes are required. Consequently, the Byzantine fault type requires more hardware for counteracting of the same number of faults. These hardware expenses increase very rapidly with increasing k (Table 3).

(c) The number of intercomputer communication rounds (Table 3) and the capacity of executed operations for the Byzantine agreement protocol

(Example 2 in Appendix I) are always more than for all of the other steps. That is why it may be written that $t_i < t_1$, where t_1 is the time period for execution of the Byzantine agreement protocol or the first step of the fault-tolerant procedure for a Byzantine fault type and t_i is the time period for execution of ith step of the fault-tolerant procedures, $i = 2, 3, 4, 5, 6$ (Table 3). Suppose that the required time period of checkpoints for counteracting of non-Byzantine fault types is defined as T_{CP}^{NB}. Then, the required time period of checkpoints for counteracting of Byzantine fault type T_{CP}^{B}, will be defined as

$$T_{CP}^{B} = T_{CP}^{NB} + t_1 \text{ , and } T_{CP}^{B} > T_{CP}^{NB} \tag{1}$$

This means that checkpoint time period for Byzantine fault type is more than for non-Byzantine fault type.

Problem #4: The Byzantine fault type indirectly decreases the degree of reliability of RCS. The fault-tolerant procedure works in checkpoints (Fig. 2). The appearance of faults in checkpoints is very dangerous because there is no mechanism to counteract them. As a result, in order to contribute to achieving "7 nines" it is necessary to decrease the probability of appearance of faults in checkpoints by shorting the time period for checkpoints. As has been noted from (1), the checkpoint time period T_{CP}^{B} for a Byzantine fault type is more than T_{CP}^{NB} for a non-Byzantine fault type. It is clear from Table 3 that T_{CP}^{B} increases very rapidly for increasing k by means of m (the required number of communication rounds). Consequently, the probability of appearance of faults in checkpoints for the Byzantine fault type is increasing and the degree of reliability is decreasing.

As we see, dealing with the Byzantine fault type is very difficult and has some important disadvantages. A key question is about the reasons for appearance of Byzantine fault type. Why does Byzantine fault type appear in RCS? Is it possible to design RCS where Byzantine fault type cannot appear? The main aims of this paper are: (1) to define the reasons of appearance of non-Byzantine and Byzantine fault types, (2) to analyze the relationship between the modes of intercomputer communications and fault types (non-Byzantine and Byzantine) in structure of RCS and (3) to suggest rules for designing of RCS in which Byzantine faults cannot appear.

4   An Analysis of Modes of Intercomputer Communications

Suppose that node n ($n = 1, 2, ..., N$) consists of a Central Processor (CP), Input Processor (IP) and Output Processor (OP) as shown in Fig. 3.

CP controls the computational process, computes its own computational result and executes the fault-tolerant procedure on the basis of computational results from all nodes in RCS. IP consists of the receivers (R1, R2, ..., RK) which receive the computational results from the other nodes. OP consists of

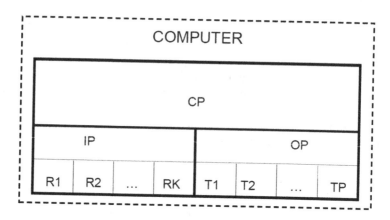

Fig. 3. The computer structure

the transmitters (T1, T2, ..., TP) which transmit the computational results to the other nodes.

The computational process executed in RCS is periodically interrupted at the checkpoints by the execution of the fault-tolerant procedure (Sect. 2.3). At checkpoints, m communication rounds are realized between nodes by the exchanging of computational results. According to the Determinate Byzantine agreement protocol, in the first communication round, each node must transmit its own computational result to all other nodes and receive the computational results from the other nodes in RCS. In the other $(m-1)$ communication round, the nodes must exchange the computational results through mediator nodes (for example, the ith node transmits to the jth node the computational result of the nth node in RCS, where $i, j, n = 1, 2, ..., N$ and $i \neq j \neq n$) (for implementation of the Determinate Byzantine agreement protocol see Example 2 in Appendix I).

Modes of intercomputer communications used for exchanging of the computational results between nodes are described in Table 4 [52–55, 75].

We will show below that fault types appearing in RCS depend on the modes described in Table 4. Intercomputer communications may be realized by using one of seven protocols (Table 5).

Example for implementation of Protocol #I: Structure of RCS with $N = 4$ for implementation of Protocol I is given in Fig. 4

According to the description of Protocol I (Table 5), $(N-1)$ communication round (CR) is required. So, for $N = 4$, $(N-1) = (4-1) = 3$ CR are needed. In any CR, OP of any computer sends the computational results to IP of corresponding computers. Namely, in the 1st CR: C1→C2 (this means that OP of the 1st computer sends the data to IP of the 2nd computer), C2→C1, C3→C4, C4→C3; in the 2nd CR: C1→C3, C3→C1, C2→C4, C4→C2 and in the 3rd CR: C1→C4, C4→C1, C2→C3, C3→C2.

Example for implementation of Protocol #II: Structure of RCS for implementation of Protocol II is the same as Protocol I (Fig. 4). According to the

Table 4. Modes of intercomputer communications

Modes of intercomputer communications	Actions executed by nodes
Broadcast Mode	The same data are transmitted from one node to all (or some) of the other connected nodes simultaneously
Time-Sharing Mode	The same data are transmitted from one node to all (or some) of the other connected nodes by using and sharing the same medium
Non-Regular Mode	Each of N nodes transmits the same data to all $(N-1)$ connected node by using $(N-1)$ transmitter in parallel, N nodes do it in sequence during N communication rounds[a]
Regular Mode	Each of N nodes transmits the same data to all $(N-1)$ connected node by using $(N-1)$ transmitter in parallel, N nodes do it in parallel during 1 communication round[a]

[a]Communication round is a time period defined by one clock pulse of the system timer.

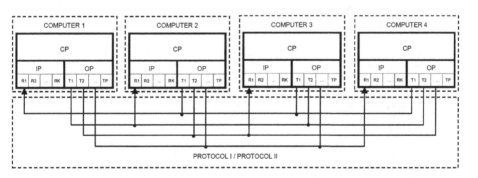

Fig. 4. Structure of RCS with $N = 4$ for implementation of Protocol #I and Protocol #II

description of Protocol II (Table 5), N communication rounds are required. So, for $N = 4$, 4 CR are needed. Namely, in the 1st CR: C1→C2, C1→C3, C1→C4; in the 2nd CR: C2→C1, C2→C3, C2→C4; in the 3rd CR: C3→C1, C3→C2, C3→C4 and in the 4th CR: C4→C1, C4→C2, C4→C3. Detailed explanation for implementation of Protocol II is given in Example 4 of Appendix I.

Table 5. Description of protocols for intercomputer communications

Protocol Number	Actions executed by OP	Actions executed by IP	Number of required communication rounds	Example Figure
I	OP of the nth node $(n = 1, 2, \ldots, N)$ transmits the computational results to IP of the ith nodes $(i = 1, 2, \ldots, N)$ and $(n \neq i)$ in the time-sharing mode by using $(N - 1)$ transmitter	IP of the nth node $(n = 1, 2, \ldots, N)$ receives the computational results from OP of the ith nodes $(i = 1, 2, \ldots, N)$ and $(n \neq i)$ in the time-sharing mode by using one receiver	All nodes execute this procedure in parallel so that for full exchange of the computational results $(N - 1)$ communication round is needed for N nodes	Fig. 4
II	OP of the nth node $(n = 1, 2, \ldots, N)$ transmits the computational results to IP of the ith nodes $(i = 1, 2, \ldots, N)$ and $(n \neq i)$ in the non-regular mode by using $(N - 1)$ transmitter in parallel	IP of the nth node $(n = 1, 2, \ldots, N)$ receives the computational results from OP of the ith nodes $(i = 1, 2, \ldots, N)$ and $(n \neq i)$ in the time-sharing mode by using one receiver	All nodes execute this procedure in sequence so that for full exchange of the computational results N communication rounds are needed for N nodes	Fig. 4
III	OP of the nth node $(n = 1, 2, \ldots, N)$ transmits the computational results to IP of the ith nodes $(i = 1, 2, \ldots, N)$ and $(n \neq i)$ in the regular mode by using $(N - 1)$ transmitter in parallel	IP of the nth node $(n = 1, 2, \ldots, N)$ receives the computational results from OP of the ith nodes $(i = 1, 2, \ldots, N)$ and $(n \neq i)$ in the regular mode by using $(N - 1)$ receiver in parallel	All nodes execute this procedure in parallel so that for full exchange of the computational results one communication round is needed for N nodes	Fig. 5
IV	OP of the nth node $(n = 1, 2, \ldots, N)$ transmits the computational results to IP of the ith nodes $(i = 1, 2, \ldots, N)$ and $(n \neq i)$ in the broadcast mode by using one transmitter	IP of the nth node $(n = 1, 2, \ldots, N)$ receives the computational results from OP of the ith nodes $(i = 1, 2, \ldots, N)$ and $(n \neq i)$ by using $(N - 1)$ receiver in parallel	All nodes execute this procedure in parallel so that for full exchange of the computational results one communication round is needed for N nodes	Fig. 6
V	OP of the nth node $(n = 1, 2, \ldots, N)$ transmits the computational results to IP of the ith nodes $(i = 1, 2, \ldots, N)$ and $(n \neq i)$ in the time sharing mode by using one transmitter	IP of the nth node $(n = 1, 2, \ldots, N)$ receives the computational results from OP of the ith nodes $(i = 1, 2, \ldots, N)$ and $(n \neq i)$ by using $(N - 1)$ receiver in sequence	All nodes execute this procedure in parallel so that for full exchange of the computational results $(N - 1)$ communication round are needed for N nodes	Fig. 6
VI	OP of the nth node $(n = 1, 2, \ldots, N)$ transmits the computational results to IP of the ith nodes $(i = 1, 2, \ldots, N)$ and $(n \neq i)$ in the time sharing mode by using one transmitter	IP of the nth node $(n = 1, 2, \ldots, N)$ receives the computational results from OP of the ith nodes $(i = 1, 2, \ldots, N)$ and $(n \neq i)$ in the time sharing mode by using one receiver	All nodes execute this procedure in sequence so that for full exchange of the computational results $3N$ communication rounds are needed for N nodes	Fig. 7
VII	OP of the nth node $(n = 1, 2, \ldots, N)$ transmits the computational results to IP of the ith nodes $(i = 1, 2, \ldots, N)$ and $(n \neq i)$ in the broadcast mode by using one transmitter	IP of the nth node $(n = 1, 2, \ldots, N)$ receives the computational results from OP of the ith nodes $(i = 1, 2, \ldots, N)$ and $(n \neq i)$ in the time sharing mode by using one receiver	All nodes execute this procedure in parallel so that for full exchange of the computational results N communication rounds are needed for N nodes	Fig. 7

Example for implementation of Protocol #III: Structure of RCS with $N = 4$ for implementation of Protocol III is given in Fig. 5.

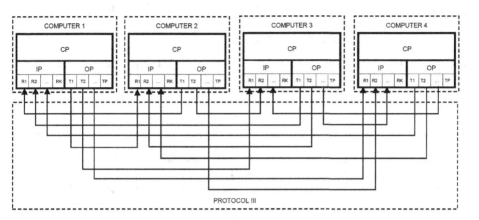

Fig. 5. Structure of RCS with $N = 4$ for implementation of Protocol #III

According to the description of Protocol III (Table 5), 1 CR is required. Namely, in the 1st CR: C1→C2, C1→C3, C1→C4, C2→C1, C2→C3, C2→C4, C3→C1, C3→C2, C3→C4, C4→C1, C4→C2, C4→C3

Example for implementation of Protocol #IV: Structure of RCS with $N = 4$ for implementation of Protocol IV is given in Fig. 6.

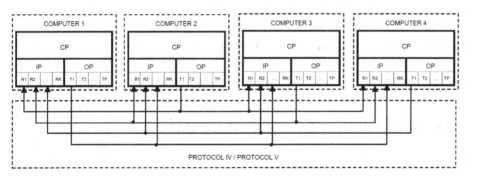

Fig. 6. Structure of RCS with $N = 4$ for implementation of Protocol #IV and Protocol #V

According to the description of Protocol IV (Table 5), 1 CR is required. Namely, in the 1st CR: C1→C2, C1→C3, C1→C4, C2→C1, C2→C3, C2→C4, C3→C1, C3→C2, C3→C4, C4→C1, C4→C2, C4→C3. Detailed explanation for implementation of Protocol IV is given in Example 4 of Appendix I.

Example for implementation of Protocol #V: Structure of RCS for implementation of Protocol V is the same as Protocol IV (Fig. 6). According to the description of Protocol V (Table 5), $(N-1)$ CR is required. So, for $N = 4$, $(N-1) = (4-1) = 3$ CR are needed. Namely, in the 1st CR: C1→C2, C2→C1, C3→C4, C4→C3; in the 2nd CR: C1→C3, C3→C1, C2→C4, C4→C2 and in the 3rd CR: C1→C4, C4→C1, C2→C3, C3→C2.

Example for implementation of Protocol #VI: Structure of RCS with $N = 4$ for implementation of Protocol VI is given in Fig. 7.

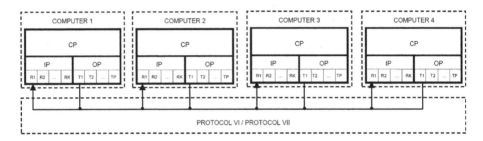

Fig. 7. Structure of RCS with $N = 4$ for implementation of Protocol #VI and Protocol #VII

According to the description of Protocol VI (Table 5), $3N$ CR are required. So, for $N = 4, 3 * N = 3 * 4 = 12$ CR are needed. Namely, in the 1st CR: C1→C2; in the 2nd CR: C1→C3; in the 3rd CR: C1→C4; in the 4th CR: C2→C1; in the 5th CR: C2→C3; in the 6th CR: C2→C4; in the 7th CR: C3→C1; in the 8th CR: C3→C2; in the 9th CR: C3→C4; in the 10th CR: C4→C1; in the 11th CR: C4→C2; in the 12th CR: C4→C3.

Example for implementation of Protocol #VII: Structure of RCS for implementation of Protocol VII is the same as Protocol VI (Fig. 7). According to the description of Protocol VII (Table 5), N communication rounds are required. So, for $N = 4$, 4 CR are needed. In the 1st CR: C1→C2, C1→C3, C1→C4; in the 2nd CR: C2→C1, C2→C3, C2→C4; in the 3rd CR: C3→C1, C3→C2, C3→C4 and in the 4th CR: C4→C1, C4→C2, C4→C3.

We consider seven protocols for RCS described above. Each of them may be realized by different schematic solutions. We do not consider the details of concrete solutions because of the length limitation.

5 An Analysis of the Relationship Between Modes of Intercomputer Communications and Fault Types

Let us analyze the relationship between the modes of intercomputer communications (described in Table 4 and used in protocols from Table 5) and the fault types (non-Byzantine and Byzantine) appeared in RCS. According to our assumption on fault appearance (Sect. 2.4) only one fault can appear in RCS during any logical segment and following checkpoint time period (the probability of the appearance of another fault is negligibly small). Suppose that the nth node in RCS is faulty. This means that fault can appear only in one of three units (IP, CP, and OP) of this node. Let us analyze these situations.

(a) Fault occurs in IP of the nth node (CP and OP are non-faulty) (Fig. 8).
    The functions of IP are to receive the computational results from the other nodes and to save them in its buffer memory. According to our assumption IP is faulty; CP and OP are non-faulty in the nth node. IP receives the computational results from the ith ($i = 1, 2, ..., N$ and $n \neq i$) node in the first and following communication rounds. Because of its faulty state, IP may continuously change the received computational results. For this reason received results will be denoted as incorrect computational results. The computational results which were received from i^{th} node to the buffer memory of the IP of the nth node and which must be resent to the IP of the jth node must be transferred from the buffer of IP to the buffer of OP of the nth node. OP transmits the same and correct computational results of CP in the first communication round and the same and incorrect computational results (which were received by IP in the first and following communication rounds) in the second and following communication rounds to the other nodes. In this case, transmitters will transmit the same computational results (it is not important whether correct or incorrect) to other nodes during all communication rounds. Consequently, the fault type is non-Byzantine.

(b) Fault occurs in CP (IP and OP are non-faulty) (Fig. 9).
    The functions of CP are to control the computational process, to compute its own computational result and to execute the fault-tolerant procedure on the basis of computational results of all nodes in RCS. According to our assumption CP is faulty; IP and OP are non-faulty in the nth node. CP

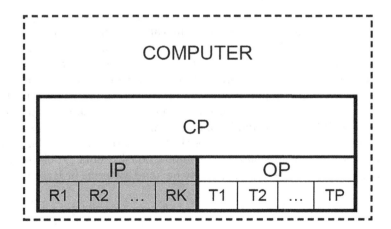

Fig. 8. Faulty state of the nth node in RCS: IP is faulty

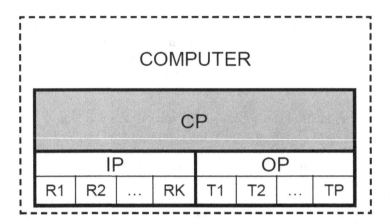

Fig. 9. Faulty state of the nth node in RCS: CP is faulty

may compute the incorrect computational result. IP receives the same and correct computational results from the other nodes in the first and following communication rounds. OP transmits the same and incorrect computational results in the first communication round and both the same and correct computational results in the second and following communication rounds. In this case, transmitters will transmit the same computational results (it is not important whether correct or incorrect) to other nodes during all communication rounds. Consequently, the fault type is non-Byzantine.

(c) Fault occurs in OP (CP and IP are non-faulty) (Fig. 10).
The main function of OP is to transmit the computational results to the other nodes. According to our assumption, OP is faulty; IP and CP are non-faulty in the nth node. IP receives the correct computational results from the ith ($i = 1, 2, ..., N$ and $n \neq i$) nodes in the first and following communication rounds. In this case, transmitters of OP will transmit the same or different (depending on the modes of intercomputer communications) computational results to other nodes during all communication rounds. Namely, transmitters of OP will transmit the same computational results (it is not important whether correct or incorrect) if the protocols IV and VII of intercomputer communications are used. According to these protocols, OP uses only broadcast mode for transmission of the computational results (Table 5). On the other hand, transmitters of OP will transmit different computational results if the protocols I, II, III, V and VI of intercomputer communications are used. According to these protocols, OP uses the time sharing, non-regular and regular modes for transmission of the computational results (Table 5). Consequently, in this case, the fault type may be non-Byzantine or Byzantine.

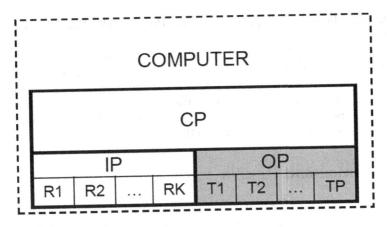

Fig. 10. Faulty state of the nth node in RCS: OP is faulty

As a result, if IP or CP is faulty it means that the fault type is exactly non-Byzantine. On the other hand, if OP is faulty it means that fault type is non-Byzantine or Byzantine depending on the protocols of intercomputer communications used in RCS (Table 6).

As shown in Table 6, the non-Byzantine and Byzantine fault types can appear in RCS with Protocol I, Protocol II (Fig. 4), Protocol III (Fig. 5), Protocol V (Fig. 6) and Protocol VI (Fig. 7). However, there are two protocols in which only

Table 6. Regular features of appeared fault types

Protocol number from Table 5	Figure Number	Appeared fault types		
		Fault occurs in IP (CP and OP are non-faulty)	Fault occurs in CP (IP and OP are non-faulty)	Fault occurs in OP (IP and CP are non-faulty)
I	Fig. 4	non-Byzantine fault can appear	non-Byzantine fault can appear	non-Byzantine and Byzantine faults can appear
II	Fig. 4	non-Byzantine fault can appear	non-Byzantine fault can appear	non-Byzantine and Byzantine faults can appear
III	Fig. 5	non-Byzantine fault can appear	non-Byzantine fault can appear	non-Byzantine and Byzantine faults can appear
IV	Fig. 6	non-Byzantine fault can appear	non-Byzantine fault can appear	non-Byzantine fault can appear
V	Fig. 6	non-Byzantine fault can appear	non-Byzantine fault can appear	non-Byzantine and Byzantine faults can appear
VI	Fig. 7	non-Byzantine fault can appear	non-Byzantine fault can appear	non-Byzantine and Byzantine faults can appear
VII	Fig. 7	non-Byzantine fault can appear	non-Byzantine fault can appear	non-Byzantine fault can appear

non-Byzantine faults can appear. These are Protocol IV (Fig. 5) and Protocol VII (Fig. 6).

In other words, (1) Faulty IP and CP cause only non-Byzantine fault type, independent of the modes of intercomputer communications used; (2) Faulty OP also causes only non-Byzantine fault type if the broadcast mode is used for transmission and (3) Faulty OP causes the non-Byzantine or Byzantine fault types if the time-sharing mode is used for transmission. So the Byzantine fault type is related only to a faulty state of OP in RCS.

6   Evaluation and Results

It is well known that there are two very important parameters for real-time control systems: reliability and performance. During the design process of such systems all actions must be focused on the following principles: (a) increasing the degree of reliability of the system in order to achieve "7 nines" and (b) decreasing the total time period for execution of the application tasks and checkpoints in order to fulfill a real-time demand. One of the ways to contribute to the execution of these principles is to design RCS that are free from Byzantine faults. In this case, the reliability and performance values achieve the maximum level (Fig. 11).

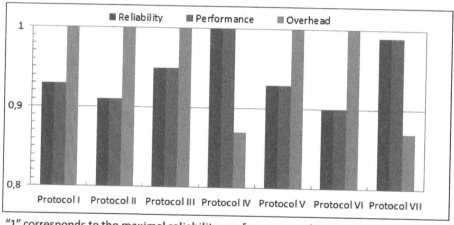

Fig. 11. Reliability, performance and overhead evaluation

The main aim of the evaluation given in Fig. 11 is to show how the Byzantine fault affects the degrees of reliability, performance and computational overhead. The following rough models were used for evaluation.

(a) Reliability evaluation:

$$R(t) = e^{-\lambda t} \tag{2}$$

where, λ is the failure rate of RCS per hour and t is a working time of RCS in hours.

The computational process executed in each node of RCS consists of a number of operating cycles (Fig. 2). Each operating cycle consists of a number of logical segments. In each logical segment, one or a certain number of application tasks is executed. After each logical segment, the checkpoint is realized. So, the processing time of RCS is defined as

$$T = T_{LS} + T_{CP} \tag{3}$$

where, T_{LS} is the total time for execution of logical segments and it is the same for all the above described protocols, T_{CP} is the total time for execution of checkpoints.

$$T_{CP} = T_{IC} + T_{FTP} \tag{4}$$

where, T_{IC} is the total time for execution of intercomputer communication rounds and T_{FTP} is the total time for execution of the fault-tolerant procedures. T_{IC} and T_{FTP} are different for all described above protocols. From Tables 3, 5 and 6,

$$T_{IC}^{III} \approx T_{IC}^{IV} < T_{IC}^{I} \approx T_{IC}^{V} < T_{IC}^{II} \approx T_{IC}^{VII} < T_{IC}^{VI} \tag{5}$$

and from Tables 1 and 6,

$$T_{FTP}^{IV} \approx T_{FTP}^{VII} < T_{FTP}^{I} \approx T_{FTP}^{II} \approx T_{FTP}^{III} \approx T_{FTP}^{V} \approx T_{FTP}^{VI} \tag{6}$$

According to (1), (5), (6) and by using (4),

$$T_{CP}^{IV} < T_{CP}^{VII} < T_{CP}^{III} < T_{CP}^{I} \approx T_{CP}^{V} < T_{CP}^{II} < T_{CP}^{VI} \tag{7}$$

Consequently, from (2),

$$R(t)^{IV} > R(t)^{VII} > R(t)^{III} > R(t)^{I} \approx R(t)^{V} > R(t)^{II} > R(t)^{VI} \tag{8}$$

According to used model, the protocols of RCS, where Byzantine faults cannot appear, have maximal degree of reliability. From Table 6 and expression (8), we see that there are two such protocols: IV and VII. Figure 11 shows that the degree of reliability of protocol IV is maximal. The protocols where Byzantine faults appear have a lower degree of reliability.

(b) Performance evaluation:

$$V = \frac{1}{T_{CP}} \tag{9}$$

According to the used model (9), the performance is increased by decreasing the time period required for checkpoints. On the basis of (7) and by using (9),

$$V^{IV} > V^{VII} > V^{III} > V^{I} \approx V^{V} > V^{II} > V^{VI} \tag{10}$$

According to the used model, the protocols of RCS where the Byzantine faults cannot appear have maximal performance. From Table 6 and expression (10), we see that there are two such protocols: IV and VII. As we see from Fig. 11, the performance of the protocol IV is maximal. The protocols where Byzantine faults can appear have lower performance.

(c) Evaluation of overhead:

Let us give rough evaluation of the overhead of maintaining of fault-tolerance. As seen from Table 1, the fault-tolerant procedure for non-Byzantine fault type consists of five steps, whereas for Byzantine fault type, it consists of six steps. Assume that all steps require equal time period (Δt) to be executed. According to this assumption the time periods of checkpoints for counteracting of non-Byzantine and Byzantine fault types will be defined as

$$T_{CP}^{NB} = 5 * \Delta t < T_{CP}^{B} = 6 * \Delta t \tag{11}$$

So, designing RCS where only non-Byzantine fault type can appear allows the designers to decrease the time period of checkpoints at least Δt time unit. In other words, the computational overhead of maintaining fault-tolerance will be reduced more than 16%.

As we can see from Fig. 11, the protocols which are free from Byzantine faults (IV and VII) have maximal degree of reliability, performance and minimal computational overhead. In addition these protocols require less software and hardware than others.

7   Conclusions

We have determined the following disadvantages: (1) the Byzantine fault type cannot be counteracted in RCS with $N = 3$; (2) during the execution of Byzantine agreement algorithms some forms of appearance of faults are masked; (3) the Byzantine fault type requires more software, hardware and processing time; (4) by means of these three disadvantages the degree of reliability of RCS is decreased and computational overhead is increased.

We have showed that there is only one way to solve these problems: that is to design RCS where Byzantine fault type cannot appear. It is better to prevent the Byzantine fault type than counteract it.

To this end, we have analyzed the relationship between the modes of intercomputer communications (such as the broadcast, time sharing, non-regular and regular modes) and the fault types (such as non-Byzantine and Byzantine) in RCS.

We have proved that the fault type appearing in RCS is defined by the modes of intercomputer communications. Byzantine fault type cannot appear in RCS if only broadcast mode is used, and non-Byzantine and Byzantine fault types can appear in RCS if the time sharing, non-regular and regular modes are used for transmission of the computational results.

We have designed the structural model of nodes and proved that the Byzantine fault can only appear when OP is faulty and when OP uses the time sharing, non-regular and regular modes of intercomputer communications.

Reliability, performance and overhead of the designed protocols were evaluated and we showed that Byzantine fault free protocols have maximal reliability and performance and minimal overhead.

This paper allows the reader to understand the disadvantages of the Byzantine fault type and to design a Byzantine fault free RCS. Designing a Byzantine fault free RCS increases the degree of reliability by preventing the masking of forms of appearance of faults and by decreasing the time period of checkpoints, and hence decreasing the probability of appearance of faults during checkpoints. Designing the Byzantine fault free RCS also increases the performance and decreases overhead by shortening of the time period of checkpoints.

Due to length consideration we give an example implementation of the paper results in Example 4 of Appendix I at the end of this manuscript.

One of future research directions is to revise the Byzantine fault problems for today's multi-core CPU and GPU accelerators using appropriate platforms such as OpenMP, OpenCL and CUDA.

Appendix I: Examples

Example 1. Let us consider a Redundant Computer System (RCS) which consists of four computers (nodes) (Fig. 1 with $N = 4$). Suppose that the fourth node is faulty and computational results of non-faulty nodes are "1". If the fourth node sends the same values, namely logical "0", to all others during the exchange by computational results it means that the fault type is Non-Byzantine.

$$\text{Node Number:} \qquad 1^{st} \qquad 2^{nd} \qquad 3^{rd} \qquad 4^{th}$$
$$\text{Vectors of Computational Results: } [1\ 1\ 1\ 0]\ [1\ 1\ 1\ 0]\ [1\ 1\ 1\ 0]\ [x\ x\ x\ x]$$

As we see, vectors consist of the same values in all non-faulty nodes. However, if the fourth node sends different values, namely to the first and third nodes logical "0" and to the second node logical "1", it means that the fault type is Byzantine.

$$\text{Node Number:} \qquad 1^{st} \qquad 2^{nd} \qquad 3^{rd} \qquad 4^{th}$$
$$\text{Vectors of Computational Results: } [1\ 1\ 1\ 0]\ [1\ 1\ 1\ 1]\ [1\ 1\ 1\ 0]\ [x\ x\ x\ x]$$

As we see, vectors consist of different values in non-faulty nodes. The index of x ("0" or "1") refers to values in faulty nodes.

Example 2. For explanation of the masking of fault forms, the Determinate Byzantine agreement protocol will be used. Suppose that $N = 4$, $k = 1$, consequently, $m = 2$ (Table 3). Let us consider the examples for three cases: (1) there is no fault in RCS; (2) the Byzantine fault appears in RCS during the first intercomputer communication round and (3) the Byzantine fault appears in RCS during the second intercomputer communication round.

Example 2.1. First, let us consider the case when there is no fault in RCS. Suppose that computational results of nodes are the logical "1".

Node Number: 1st 2nd 3rd 4th
Computational Results: 1   1   1   1

In the first intercomputer communication round, nodes exchange the computational results. So after the first round, the following vectors are formed.

Node Number: 1st 2nd 3rd 4th
Vectors of Computational Results: $\begin{bmatrix}1\,1\,1\,1\end{bmatrix}$ $\begin{bmatrix}1\,1\,1\,1\end{bmatrix}$ $\begin{bmatrix}1\,1\,1\,1\end{bmatrix}$ $\begin{bmatrix}1\,1\,1\,1\end{bmatrix}$

In the second intercomputer communication round, the ith node transmits to the jth node the computational result of the nth node, where i, j, $n = 1, 2, 3, 4$ and $i \neq j \neq n$. After the second round, the matrices of the computational results are formed.

Node Number: 1st 2nd 3rd 4th

Matrices of
Computational Results:
$$\begin{bmatrix}1&.&.&.\\.&1&1&1\\.&1&1&1\\.&1&1&1\end{bmatrix} \begin{bmatrix}1&.&1&1\\.&1&.&.\\1&.&1&1\\1&.&1&1\end{bmatrix} \begin{bmatrix}1&1&.&1\\1&1&.&1\\.&.&1&.\\1&1&.&1\end{bmatrix} \begin{bmatrix}1&1&1&.\\1&1&1&.\\1&1&1&.\\.&.&.&1\end{bmatrix}$$

After majority voting in columns, the final vectors are formed. Element a_{nn} is chosen as majority of values in the nth column, where $n = 1, 2, 3, 4$.

Node Number: 1st 2nd 3rd 4th
Final Vectors: $\begin{bmatrix}1\,1\,1\,1\end{bmatrix}$ $\begin{bmatrix}1\,1\,1\,1\end{bmatrix}$ $\begin{bmatrix}1\,1\,1\,1\end{bmatrix}$ $\begin{bmatrix}1\,1\,1\,1\end{bmatrix}$

As we see, all matrices consist of the same computational results and all nodes forms the same final vectors. This means that there is no fault in RCS.

Example 2.2. Now, let us consider the case when the Byzantine fault appears in the first intercomputer communication round. Suppose that the fourth node is faulty and computational results of nodes are the logical "1", "1", "1", "x" ("0" or "1").

Node Number: 1st 2nd 3rd 4th
Computational Results: 1   1   1   x

Suppose that the faulty node sends to the first and third nodes the logical "0" and to the second node the logical "1" during the first intercomputer communication round. After the first round, the following vectors are formed.

Node Number: 1st 2nd 3rd 4th
Vectors of Computational Results: $\begin{bmatrix}1\,1\,1\,0\end{bmatrix}$ $\begin{bmatrix}1\,1\,1\,1\end{bmatrix}$ $\begin{bmatrix}1\,1\,1\,0\end{bmatrix}$ $\begin{bmatrix}x\,x\,x\,x\end{bmatrix}$

After the second round, the following matrices and after majority voting in columns, the following final vectors are formed.

Node Number: 1st 2nd 3rd 4th

Matrices of
Computational Results:
$$\begin{bmatrix} 1 & . & . & . \\ . & 1 & 1 & x \\ . & 1 & 1 & x \\ . & 1 & 0 & 0 \end{bmatrix} \begin{bmatrix} 1 & . & 1 & x \\ . & 1 & . & . \\ 1 & . & 1 & x \\ 0 & . & 0 & 1 \end{bmatrix} \begin{bmatrix} 1 & 1 & . & x \\ 1 & 1 & . & x \\ . & . & 1 & . \\ 0 & 1 & . & 0 \end{bmatrix} \begin{bmatrix} x & x & x & . \\ x & x & x & . \\ x & x & x & . \\ . & . & . & x \end{bmatrix}$$

Node Number: 1st 2nd 3rd 4th
Vectors of Computational Results: $\begin{bmatrix} 1 & 1 & 1 & x \end{bmatrix}$ $\begin{bmatrix} 1 & 1 & 1 & x \end{bmatrix}$ $\begin{bmatrix} 1 & 1 & 1 & x \end{bmatrix}$ $\begin{bmatrix} x & x & x & x \end{bmatrix}$

As we see, the matrices in all non-faulty nodes consist of different computational results. However, all non-faulty nodes form the same final vectors, where the fourth computational result differs from others. So the non-faulty nodes determine that the fourth node is faulty. In this case, the Determinate Byzantine agreement algorithm transforms the Byzantine fault type appearing in the first intercomputer communication round to Non-Byzantine type.

Example 2.3. Finally, let us consider the case when the Byzantine fault appears in the second intercomputer communication round. Suppose that the computational results of nodes are the logical "1".

Node Number: 1st 2nd 3rd 4th
Computational Results: 1   1   1   1

After the first round, the following vectors are formed.

Node Number: 1st 2nd 3rd 4th
Vectors of Computational Results: $\begin{bmatrix} 1 & 1 & 1 & 1 \end{bmatrix}$ $\begin{bmatrix} 1 & 1 & 1 & 1 \end{bmatrix}$ $\begin{bmatrix} 1 & 1 & 1 & 1 \end{bmatrix}$ $\begin{bmatrix} 1 & 1 & 1 & 1 \end{bmatrix}$

Suppose that the Byzantine fault appears in the fourth node during the second intercomputer communication round. The faulty node will send different computational results to the non-faulty nodes. After the second round, the following matrices are formed.

Node Number: 1st 2nd 3rd 4th

Matrices of
Computational Results:
$$\begin{bmatrix} 1 & . & . & . \\ . & 1 & 1 & 1 \\ . & 1 & 1 & 0 \\ . & 1 & 1 & 1 \end{bmatrix} \begin{bmatrix} 1 & . & 1 & 0 \\ . & 1 & . & . \\ 1 & . & 1 & 1 \\ 1 & . & 1 & 1 \end{bmatrix} \begin{bmatrix} 1 & 1 & . & 0 \\ 1 & 1 & . & 1 \\ . & . & 1 & . \\ 1 & 1 & . & 1 \end{bmatrix} \begin{bmatrix} 1 & 1 & 1 & . \\ 1 & 1 & 1 & . \\ 1 & 1 & 1 & . \\ . & . & . & 1 \end{bmatrix}$$

After majority voting in columns, the following final vectors are formed.

Node Number: 1st 2nd 3rd 4th
Final Vectors: $\begin{bmatrix} 1 & 1 & 1 & 1 \end{bmatrix}$ $\begin{bmatrix} 1 & 1 & 1 & 1 \end{bmatrix}$ $\begin{bmatrix} 1 & 1 & 1 & 1 \end{bmatrix}$ $\begin{bmatrix} 1 & 1 & 1 & 1 \end{bmatrix}$

As we see, the matrices in all non-faulty nodes consist of different computational results. Despite this, all non-faulty nodes form the same final vectors where all computational results are the same. The non-faulty nodes determine that there is no fault in RCS. This means that the Determinate Byzantine agreement algorithm masks the Byzantine fault type that appeared in the second round. The same situation will take place when the Non-Byzantine fault appears in RCS during the second intercomputational round. As result, the Byzantine agreement algorithms mask the Non-Byzantine and Byzantine fault appearance forms that occurred during the second and following rounds. Masking of faults is very dangerous because they can be accumulated and lead the system to failure.

Example 3. Let us show that the use of a Byzantine agreement algorithm (for example, the Determinate Byzantine agreement algorithm) cannot counteract the Byzantine fault in RCS with $N = 3$ (Fig. 1 with $N = 3$). Suppose that the third node is faulty and computational results of nodes are "1", "1", "x" ("0" or "1").

Node Number: 1st 2nd 3rd
Computational Results: 1   1   x

Suppose that the faulty node sends to the first node the logical "0" and to the second node the logical "1" during the first intercomputer communication round. So after the first round, the following vectors are formed.

Node Number: 1st 2nd 3rd
Vectors of
Computational Results: $\begin{bmatrix} 1 & 1 & 0 \end{bmatrix}$ $\begin{bmatrix} 1 & 1 & 1 \end{bmatrix}$ $\begin{bmatrix} x & x & x \end{bmatrix}$

After the second round, the following matrices are formed.

Node Number: 1st 2nd 3rd
Matrices of Computational Results: $\begin{bmatrix} 1 & . & . \\ . & 1 & x \\ . & 1 & 0 \end{bmatrix}$ $\begin{bmatrix} 1 & . & x \\ . & 1 & . \\ 0 & . & 1 \end{bmatrix}$ $\begin{bmatrix} x & x & . \\ x & x & . \\ . & . & x \end{bmatrix}$

After majority voting in columns, the following final vectors are formed. As we see, all non-faulty nodes form the different final vectors and could not determine the faulty node. So the Byzantine agreement algorithms cannot detect the Byzantine fault in RCS with $N = 3$.

Node Number: 1st 2nd 3rd
Final Vectors: $\begin{bmatrix} 1 & 1 & ? \end{bmatrix}$ $\begin{bmatrix} ? & 1 & ? \end{bmatrix}$ $\begin{bmatrix} x & x & x \end{bmatrix}$

Example 4. Let us consider RCS where Non-Byzantine and Byzantine fault types may occur (Fig. 12).

Suppose that the nth ($n = 1, 2, 3, 4$) computer (node) in RCS consists of Central Processor (CP), Input Processor (IP) and Output Processor (OP) as shown in Fig. 12.

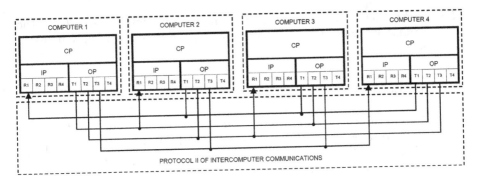

Fig. 12. Example for RCS using Protocol #II

Each CP controls its own computational process, computes its own computational result and executes its own fault-tolerant procedure on the basis of IDS which consists of computational results of all nodes in RCS. Each IP consists of 4 receivers ($R1$, $R2$, $R3$, and $R4$) which receive the computational results from the other nodes. Each OP consists of 4 transmitters ($T1$, $T2$, $T3$, and $T4$) which transmit the computational results to the other nodes.

On the one hand, in this protocol, OP of the nth node ($n = 1, 2, 3, 4$) transmits the computational results to IP of the ith nodes ($i = 1, 2, 3, 4$ and $n \neq i$) in parallel, by using three busses. Nodes execute this procedure in sequential order by using three busses in the time-sharing mode. For example:

- $T1$, $T2$ and $T3$ of OP of the 1st node transmit the computational result in the instant of time t_1 to other nodes by using three busses in parallel;
- $T1$, $T2$ and $T3$ of OP of the 2nd node transmit the computational result in instant of time t_2 to other nodes by using three busses in parallel;
- $T1$, $T2$ and $T3$ of OP of the 3rd node transmit the computational result in instant of time t_3 to other nodes by using three busses in parallel;
- $T1$, $T2$ and $T3$ of OP of the 4th node transmit computational result in instant of time t_4 to other nodes by using three busses in parallel.

On the other hand, in this protocol, IP of the nth node ($n = 1, 2, 3, 4$) receives the computational results from OP of the ith nodes ($i = 1, 2, 3, 4$ and $n \neq i$) in the time-sharing mode by using one bus. All nodes execute this procedure in parallel. For example:

- $R1$ of IP of the 1st node receives the computational results from $T1$ of the 2nd, 3rd and 4th nodes in instants of times t_1, t_3 and t_4 accordingly by using one bus;
- $R1$ of IP of the 2nd node receives the computational results from $T1$ of the 1st node and from $T2$ of 3rd and 4th nodes in instants of times t_1, t_3 and t_4 accordingly by using one bus;
- $R1$ of IP of the 3rd node receives the computational results from $T2$ of the 1st and 2nd nodes and from $T3$ of the 4th node in instants of times t_1, t_2 and t_4 accordingly by using one bus;

- *R1* of IP of the 4th node receives the computational results from *T3* of the 1st, 2nd and 3rd nodes in instants of times t_1, t_2 and t_3 accordingly by using one bus.

We assume that only one fault may occur in RCS in any instant of time (Sect. 2.4). According to this assumption, three cases may take place:

(1) Fault occurs in IP (CP and OP are non-faulty) of the nth node. The functions of IP are to receive the computational results from the other nodes and to save them in its buffer memory. According to assumption if IP is faulty, CP and OP are non-faulty in the nth ($n = 1, 2, 3, 4$) node.

  - Faulty IP may change the received correct computational results from the ith ($i = 1, 2, 3, 4$ and $n \neq i$) nodes in the first and following communication rounds and save correct or incorrect computational results in its buffer memory.
  - Non-faulty CP computes its own correct computational result.
  - Non-faulty OP transmits the same (correct) computational result (which is computed in non-faulty CP and which was not received and changed by faulty IP) in the first communication round and the same (possibly correct or incorrect) computational results (which were received and may be changed by faulty IP in the first and following communication rounds) in the second and the following communication rounds to the other nodes.

In this case, transmitters of non-faulty OP will transmit the same computational results (it is not important whether it is correct or incorrect) to other nodes during all communication rounds. Consequently, if a fault occurs in IP, the type of appeared faults in the above RCS structure is only Non-Byzantine.

(2) Fault occurs in CP (IP and OP are non-faulty) of the nth node. The functions of CP are to control its own computational process, to compute its own computational result and to execute its own fault-tolerant procedure on the basis of IDS which consists of computational results of all nodes in RCS. According to our assumption, if CP is faulty, IP and OP are non-faulty in the nth node.

  - Non-faulty IP receives the same (correct) computational results from the other nodes in the first and following communication rounds.
  - Faulty CP may compute its own incorrect computational result.
  - Non-faulty OP transmits the same (may be correct or incorrect) computational result (which is computed in faulty CP of the nth node) in the first communication round and the same (correct) computational results (which were received by non-faulty IP in the first and the following communication rounds) in the second and following communication rounds.

In this case, transmitters will also transmit the same computational results (it is not important whether it is correct or incorrect) to other nodes during all communication rounds. Consequently, if fault occurs in CP, the type of appeared faults in the above mentioned RCS structure is also only Non-Byzantine.

(3) Fault occurs in OP (CP and IP are non-faulty) of the nth node. The main function of OP is to transmit the computational results to the other nodes. According to our assumption, if OP is faulty, IP and CP are non-faulty in the nth node.

  - Non-faulty IP receives the correct computational results from the other nodes in the first and following communication rounds.
  - Non-faulty CP computes its own correct computational result.
  - Faulty OP might transmit the different computational results to other nodes during all communication rounds because OP has multiple transmitters (in this case three of them are used) for transmission and one or more of them might be faulty and may change the transmitted values.

Consequently, if fault occurs in OP, the type of appeared faults in the above RCS structure is Non-Byzantine or Byzantine.

Let us change the connections between nodes in RCS in Fig. 12 so that the Byzantine fault type could not occur (Fig. 13).

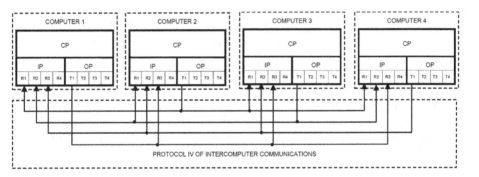

Fig. 13. Example for RCS using Protocol #IV (Byzantine fault free protocol)

On the one hand, in this protocol, only one transmitter of OP of the nth node ($n = 1, 2, 3, 4$) transmits the computational result to IP of all other nodes in the broadcast mode by using one bus simultaneously. Nodes execute this procedure in sequence. For example:

  - *T1* of OP of the 1st node transmits the computational result in instant of time t_1 to other nodes in the broadcast mode by using one bus simultaneously;
  - *T1* of OP of the 2nd node transmits the computational result in instant of time t_2 to other nodes in the broadcast mode by using one bus simultaneously;
  - *T1* of OP of the 3rd node transmits the computational result in instant of time t_3 to other nodes in the broadcast mode by using one bus simultaneously;
  - *T1* of OP of the 4th node transmits the computational result in instant of time t_4 to other nodes in the broadcast mode by using one bus simultaneously;

On the other hand, IP of the nth node ($n = 1, 2, 3, 4$) receives the computational results from OP of the ith nodes ($i = 1, 2, 3, 4$ and $n \neq i$) by using (N-1) bus in sequential order. All nodes execute this procedure in parallel. For example:

- $R1$, $R2$ and $R3$ of IP of the 1st node receive the computational result from 2nd, 3rd and 4th nodes in instants of times t_2, t_3 and t_4 accordingly by using three different busses;
- $R1$, $R2$ and $R3$ of IP of the 2nd node receive the computational result from 1st, 3rd and 4th nodes in instants of times t_1, t_3 and t_4 accordingly by using three different busses;
- $R1$, $R2$ and $R3$ of IP of the 3rd node receive the computational result from 1st, 2nd and 4th nodes in instants of times t_1, t_2 and t_4 accordingly by using three different busses;
- $R1$, $R2$ and $R3$ of IP of the 4th node receive the computational result from 1st, 2nd and 3rd nodes in instants of times t_1, t_2 and t_3 accordingly by using three different busses;

According to the assumption, three cases are also possible here. Discussions about the first and second cases are the same as for the previous protocol. The difference is in the third case in which the transmitter of faulty OP transmits the same computational results (it is not important whether correct or incorrect) because of the used broadcast mode.

Consequently, if a fault occurs in OP, the type of faults appearing in the RCS structure will only be ***Non-Byzantine***.

As a result, we changed the connections between nodes and got RCS where only Non-Byzantine fault type might occur. Consequently, by changing connection modes between nodes we can block the occurrence of the Byzantine fault type in RCS.

References

1. Avizienis, A., Laprie, J.C., Randell, B., Landwehr, C.: Basic concepts and taxonomy of dependable and secure computing. IEEE Trans. Dependable Secur. Comput. **1**(1), 11–33 (2004)
2. Bentley, J.: Introduction to Reliability and Quality Engineering. Addison-Wesley, Reading (1999)
3. Pradhan, D.K. (ed.): Fault-tolerant Computer System Design. Prentice-Hall Inc., Upper Saddle River (1996)
4. Kwak, S.W., Choi, B.J., Kim, B.K.: An optimal checkpointing-strategy for real-time control systems under transient faults. IEEE Trans. Reliab. **50**(3), 293–301 (2001)
5. Zhang, Y., Jiang, J.: Integrated active fault-tolerant control using IMM approach. IEEE Trans. Aerosp. Electron. Syst. **37**(4), 1221–1235 (2001)
6. Alvisi, L., Malkhi, D., Pierce, E., Reiter, M.K.: Fault detection for Byzantine quorum systems. IEEE Trans. Parallel Distrib. Syst. **12**(9), 996–1007 (2001)
7. Lamport, L., Shostak, R., Pease, M.: The Byzantine generals problem. ACM Trans. Program. Lang. Syst. **4**(3), 382–401 (1982)

8. Lima, G.M., Burns, A.: A consensus protocol for CAN-based systems. In: 24th IEEE Real-Time Systems Symposium, RTSS 2003, pp. 420–429. IEEE (2003)
9. Cristian, F., Aghili, H., Strong, R., Dolev, D.: Atomic broadcast: from simple message diffusion to Byzantine agreement. Inf. Comput. **118**(1), 158–179 (1995)
10. Pelc, A., Peleg, D.: Broadcasting with locally bounded Byzantine faults. Inf. Process. Lett. **93**(3), 109–115 (2005)
11. Fitzi, M., Gottesman, D., Hirt, M., Holenstein, T., Smith, A.: Detectable Byzantine agreement secure against faulty majorities. In: Proceedings of the Twenty-First Annual Symposium on Principles of Distributed Computing, pp. 118–126. ACM (2002)
12. Fitzi, M., Hirt, M.: Optimally efficient multi-valued Byzantine agreement. In: Proceedings of the Twenty-Fifth Annual ACM Symposium on Principles of Distributed Computing, pp. 163–168. ACM (2006)
13. Bao, F., Igarishi, Y.: Reliable broadcasting in product networks with Byzantine faults. In: Proceedings of Annual Symposium on Fault Tolerant Computing, pp. 262–271. IEEE (1996)
14. Keichafer, R.M., Walter, C.J., Finn, A.M., Thambidurai, P.M.: The MAFT architecture for distributed fault tolerance. IEEE Trans. Comput. **37**(4), 398–404 (1988)
15. Powell, D., Arlat, J., Beus-Dukic, L., Bondavalli, A., Coppola, P., Fantechi, A., Jenn, E., Rabejac, C., Wellings, A.: GUARDS: a generic upgradable architecture for real-time dependable systems. IEEE Trans. Parallel Distrib. Syst. **10**(6), 580–599 (1999)
16. Totel, E., Beus-Dukic, L., Blanquart, J.P., Deswarte, Y., Powell, D., Wellings, A.: Integrity management in GUARDS. In: Davies, N., Jochen, S., Raymond, K. (eds.) Middleware 1998, pp. 105–122. Springer, London (1998)
17. Palumbo, D.L., Butler, R.W.: A performance evaluation of the software-implemented fault-tolerance computer. J. Guidance Control Dyn. **9**(2), 175–180 (1986)
18. Hopkins, A.L., Smith, T.B., Lala, J.H.: FTMP: a highly reliable fault-tolerant multiprocess for aircraft. Proc. IEEE **66**(10), 1221–1239 (1978)
19. Han, S., Shin, K.G.: Experimental evaluation of failure-detection schemes in real-time communication networks. In: Twenty-Seventh Annual International Symposium on Fault-Tolerant Computing, FTCS-27, Digest of Papers, pp. 122–131. IEEE (1997)
20. Rufino, J., Verissimo, P., Arroz, G., Almeida, C., Rodrigues, L.: Fault-tolerant broadcasts in CAN. In: Twenty-Eighth Annual International Symposium on Fault-Tolerant Computing, Digest of Papers, pp. 150–159. IEEE (1998)
21. AlMohammad, B., Bose, B.: Fault-tolerant communication algorithms in toroidal networks. IEEE Trans. Parallel Distrib. Syst. **10**(10), 976–983 (1999)
22. Hsieh, H.C., Chiang, M.L.: A new solution for the Byzantine agreement problem. J. Parallel Distrib. Comput. **71**(10), 1261–1277 (2011)
23. Saini, P., Singh, A.K.: An efficient Byzantine fault tolerant agreement. In: AIP Conference Proceedings, vol. 1324, no. 1 (2010)
24. Wang, S.S., Yan, K.Q., Wang, S.C.: An optimal solution for Byzantine agreement under a hierarchical cluster-oriented mobile ad hoc network. Comput. Electr. Eng. **36**(1), 100–113 (2010)
25. Moniz, H., Neves, N.F., Correia, M.: Byzantine fault-tolerant consensus in wireless ad hoc networks. IEEE Trans. Mobile Comput. **12**(12), 2441–2454 (2013)
26. Veronese, G.S., Correia, M., Bessani, A.N., Lung, L.C., Verissimo, P.: Efficient Byzantine fault-tolerance. IEEE Trans. Comput. **62**(1), 16–30 (2013)

27. Kotla, R., Clement, A., Wong, E., Alvisi, L., Dahlin, M.: Zyzzyva: speculative Byzantine fault tolerance. Commun. ACM **51**(11), 86–95 (2008)
28. Keidar, I., Rajsbaum, S.: On the cost of fault-tolerant consensus when there are no faults: preliminary version. SIGACT News **32**(2), 45–63 (2001)
29. Banu, N., Izumi, T., Wada, K.: Adaptive and doubly-expedited one-step consensus in Byzantine asynchronous systems. Parallel Process. Lett. **21**(04), 461–477 (2011)
30. Patra, A., Choudhury, A., Rangan, C.P.: Asynchronous Byzantine agreement with optimal resilience. Distrib. Comput. **27**(2), 111–146 (2014)
31. Xu, X., Lin, Y.: Checkpoint selection in fault recovery based on Byzantine fault model. In: Fourth International Conference on Computational Intelligence and Communication Networks (CICN), pp. 582–587, November 2012
32. Widder, J., Biely, M., Gridling, G., Weiss, B., Blanquart, J.P.: Consensus in the presence of mortal Byzantine faulty processes. Distrib. Comput. **24**(6), 299–321 (2012)
33. Wang, S.C., Yan, K.Q., Ho, C.L., Wang, S.S.: The optimal generalized Byzantine agreement in cluster-based wireless sensor networks. Comput. Stan. Interfaces **36**(5), 821–830 (2014)
34. Abdelhakim, M., Lightfoot, L.E., Ren, J., Li, T.: Distributed detection in mobile access wireless sensor networks under Byzantine attacks. IEEE Trans. Parallel Distrib. Syst. **25**(4), 950–959 (2014)
35. Duran, A., Ferrer, R., Costa, J.J., Gonzàlez, M., Martorell, X., Ayguadé, E., Labarta, J.: A proposal for error handling in OpenMP. Int. J. Parallel Prog. **35**(4), 393–416 (2007)
36. Bronevetsky, G., Marques, D., Pingali, K., Szwed, P., Schulz, M.: Application-level checkpointing for shared memory programs. In: Proceedings of the 11th International Conference on Architectural Support for Programming Languages and Operating Systems. ASPLOS XI, pp. 235–247. ACM, New York (2004)
37. Bronevetsky, G., Pingali, K., Stodghill, P.: Experimental evaluation of application-level checkpointing for OpenMP programs. In: Proceedings of the 20th Annual International Conference on Supercomputing, ICS 2006, pp. 2–13. ACM, New York (2006)
38. Fu, H., Ding, Y.: Using redundant threads for fault tolerance of OpenMP programs. In: 2010 International Conference on Information Science and Applications, pp. 1–8, April 2010
39. Li, M., Hsiao, M.S.: 3-D parallel fault simulation with GPGPU. IEEE Trans. Comput. Aided Design Integr. Circuits Syst. **30**(10), 1545–1555 (2011)
40. Guo, X., Jiang, H., Li, K.C.: A checkpoint/restart scheme for CUDA applications with complex memory hierarchy. In: 14th ACIS International Conference on Software Engineering, Artificial Intelligence, Networking and Parallel/Distributed Computing (SNPD), pp. 247–252, July 2013
41. Carlo, S.D., Gambardella, G., Martella, I., Prinetto, P., Rolfo, D., Trotta, P.: Fault mitigation strategies for CUDA GPUs. In: 2013 IEEE International Test Conference (ITC), pp. 1–8, September 2013
42. Xu, X.H., Yang, X.J., Xue, J.L., Lin, Y.F., Lin, Y.S.: PartialRC: a partial recomputing method for efficient fault recovery on GPGPUs. J. Comput. Sci. Technol. **27**(2), 240–255 (2012)
43. Laosooksathit, S., Nassar, R., Leangsuksun, C., Paun, M.: Reliability-aware performance model for optimal GPU-enabled cluster environment. J. Supercomputing **68**(3), 1630–1651 (2014)
44. Demchik, V., Kolomoyets, N.: QCDGPU: open-source package for Monte Carlo lattice simulations on OpenCL-compatible multi-GPU systems (2013)

45. Avizienis, A.: Fault-tolerance: a property that ensures constant availability of digital system. IEEE Trans. Comput. **66**(10), 5–25 (1978)
46. Pease, M., Shostak, R., Lamport, L.: Reaching agreement in the presence of faults. J. ACM **27**(2), 228–234 (1980)
47. Mamedli, È.M., Samedov, R.Y., Sobolev, N.: A method for localization of Byzantine and nonbyzantine faults. Avtomatika i Telemekhanika **5**, 126–138 (1992)
48. Samet, R.: Recovery device for real-time dual-redundant computer systems. IEEE Trans. Dependable Secure Comput. **8**(3), 391–403 (2011)
49. Samet, R.: Choosing between design options for real-time computers tolerating a single fault. J. Circuits Syst. Comput. **19**(05), 1041–1068 (2010)
50. Sivencrona, H., Johannessen, P., Persson, M., Torin, J.: Heavy-ion fault injections in the time-triggered communication protocol. In: Lemos, R., Weber, T.S., Camargo, J.B. (eds.) LADC 2003. LNCS, vol. 2847, pp. 69–80. Springer, Heidelberg (2003). doi:10.1007/978-3-540-45214-0_8
51. Driscoll, K., Hall, B., Sivencrona, H., Zumsteg, P.: Byzantine fault tolerance, from theory to reality. In: Anderson, S., Felici, M., Littlewood, B. (eds.) SAFECOMP 2003. LNCS, vol. 2788, pp. 235–248. Springer, Heidelberg (2003). doi:10.1007/978-3-540-39878-3_19
52. Tanenbaum, A.S.: Computer Networks, vol. 3. Prentice Hall, New Jersey (1996)
53. Stallings, W.: Data and computer communications. Pearson/Prentice Hall (2007)
54. Mullender, S.: Distributed Systems. ACM Press/Addison-Wesley Publishing Co. (1993)
55. Coulouris, G.F., Dollimore, J., Kindberg, T.: Distributed Systems: Concepts and Design. Pearson education (2005)
56. Mitra, S., Saxena, N.R., McCluskey, E.J.: A design diversity metric and analysis of redundant systems. IEEE Trans. Comput. **51**(5), 498–510 (2002)
57. Samedov, R.: An approach to the support of the fault-tolerance of the double redundant computer control systems. Math. Comput. Appl. **4**(2), 175–184 (1999)
58. Kim, H., Jeon, H.J., Lee, K., Lee, H.: The design and evaluation of all voting triple modular redundancy system. In: Proceedings. Annual Reliability and Maintainability Symposium, pp. 439–444. IEEE (2002)
59. Smith, T.B.: Fault tolerant processor concepts and operation. In: Digest of Papers, FTCS-14, Kissimmee, USA, pp. 158–163 (1984)
60. Laprie, J.C.: Dependable computing and fault-tolerance. In: Digest of Papers FTCS-15, pp. 2–11 (1985)
61. Mamedli, È.M., Samedov, R.Y., Sobolev, N.: A method for localization of Byzantine and NonByzantine faults. J. Autom. Remote Control **53**(5), 734–744 (1992)
62. Oh, N., Mitra, S., McCluskey, E.J.: ED4I: error detection by diverse data and duplicated instructions. IEEE Trans. Comput. **51**(2), 180–199 (2002)
63. Siewiorek, D.P., Swarz, R.S.: Reliable Computer Systems: Design and Evaluation, 3rd edn. A.K. Peters Ltd., Natick (1998)
64. Samet, R.: Fault-tolerant procedures for redundant computer systems. Qual. Reliab. Eng. Int. **25**(1), 41–68 (2009)
65. Hurst, S.L.: VLSI Testing: digital and mixed analogue/digital techniques, vol. 9. IET (1998)
66. Lala, P.K.: Self-checking and fault-tolerant digital design. Morgan Kaufmann (2001)
67. Powell, D.: Failure mode assumptions and assumption coverage. In: Randell, B., Laprie, J.C., Kopetz, H., Littlewood, B. (eds.) Predictably Dependable Computing Systems, pp. 123–140. Springer, Heidelberg (1995)

68. Laprie, J.C., Arlat, J., Blanquart, J., Costes, A., Crouzet, Y., Deswarte, Y., Fabre, J., Guillermain, H., Kaâniche, M., Kanoun, K., et al.: Guide de la sûreté de fonctionnement (dependability handbook). Cépaduès, Toulouse (1995)
69. Ziv, A., Bruck, J.: An on-line algorithm for checkpoint placement. IEEE Trans. Comput. **46**(9), 976–985 (1997)
70. Ling, Y., Mi, J., Lin, X.: A variational calculus approach to optimal checkpoint placement. IEEE Trans. Comput. **50**(7), 699–708 (2001)
71. Lincoln, P., Rushby, J.: A formally verified algorithm for interactive consistency under a hybrid fault model. In: The Twenty-Third International Symposium on Fault-Tolerant Computing, FTCS-23, Digest of Papers, pp. 402–411. IEEE (1993)
72. Meyer, F.J., Pradhan, D.K.: Consensus with dual failure modes. IEEE Trans. Parallel Distrib. Syst. **2**(2), 214–222 (1991)
73. Thambidurai, P., Park, Y.K.: Interactive consistency with multiple failure modes. In: Proceedings, Seventh Symposium on Reliable Distributed Systems, pp. 93–100. IEEE (1988)
74. Chor, B., Coan, B.A.: A simple and efficient randomized Byzantine agreement algorithm. IEEE Trans. Softw. Eng. **6**, 531–539 (1985)
75. Kopetz, H.: Real-Time Systems: Design Principles for Distributed Embedded Applications. Springer Science & Business Media, London (2011)

Efficient Circuit Design of Reversible Square

H.V. Jayashree[1], Himanshu Thapliyal[2(✉)], and Vinod Kumar Agrawal[3]

[1] Department of Electronics and Communication Engineering,
PES Institute of Technology, Bengaluru 560085, Karnataka, India
jayashreehv@pes.edu
[2] Department of Electrical and Computer Engineering,
University of Kentucky, Lexington, KY 40506, USA
hthapliyal@uky.edu
[3] Department of Information Science and Engineering, PES Institute of Technology,
Bengaluru 560085, Karnataka, India
vk.agrawal@pes.edu

Abstract. In the midst of emerging technology, reversible computing is promising due to its application in the field of quantum computing. The computing hardware plays a significant role in digital signal processing (DSP) and multimedia application; one such major computing hardware is multiplier. It is a practice to choose multiplier to compute square of an operand. Multiplication hardware requires more elementary computations which leads to performance degradation in terms of reversible performance metrics like quantum cost, garbage outputs, and ancilla inputs. Ancilla inputs and garbage outputs are overhead bits in a reversible circuit. Reversible quantum computers of many qubits are extremely difficult to realize, thus we propose garbageless circuit design for reversible square computation. The proposed design methodology is based on recursion. Recursion technique is adapted from Karatsuba's recursive method to compute square of an operand; we designed inverse computation units to retrieve the inputs and obtain garbageless circuit. On comparing proposed circuit design with existing reversible square designs and Karatsuba multiplier design, we observed that our work improves number of input lines which includes data lines and ancilla lines.

Keywords: Garbageless square · Reversible circuit · Ancilla inputs

1 Introduction

Reversible logic is emerging as a promising computing paradigm with applications in ultra-low power green computing and emerging nano technologies such as quantum computing, quantum dot cellular automata (QCA), optical computing, etc. Reversible circuits are similar to conventional logic circuits except that they are built from reversible gates [2]. In reversible gates, there is a unique, one-to-one mapping between the inputs and outputs, not the case with conventional logic. The most promising applications of reversible logic lies in quantum computing since quantum circuit is a network of quantum gates. Each gate performs

© Springer-Verlag GmbH Germany 2017
M.L. Gavrilova and C.J. Kenneth Tan (Eds.): Trans. on Comput. Sci. XXIX, LNCS 10220, pp. 33–46, 2017.
DOI: 10.1007/978-3-662-54563-8_2

unitary operation on qubits which represents elementary unit of information. Qubits corresponds to conventional binary bits 0 and 1. Qubits are allowed to be in superposition of both the states 0 and 1. These unitary operations are reversible, hence quantum circuits are built using reversible logic gates.

While designing reversible circuit, several performance measuring parameters need to be considered such as quantum cost, garbage outputs, and ancilla input bits. The quantum cost of a reversible circuit is the number of 1×1 and 2×2 reversible gates used in its design; it can be considered equivalent to number of transistors needed in a conventional CMOS design. The garbage output refers to the output which exists in the circuit to maintain one-to-one mapping but is not a primary or a useful output. The constant inputs (0 or 1) are called ancilla bits which are used in reversible circuits for storing intermediate values during computation. Reversible computers including quantum computers of many bits are extremely difficult to realize, so the number of ancilla inputs and the garbage outputs in the reversible circuits need to be minimized. While designing reversible circuits, one needs to optimize these parameters to improve the footprint of the overall design. Arithmetic units are the key components of computing systems. Therefore, researchers have concentrated their efforts towards the design of reversible quantum adders [15,19,22], [4,6,13], [3,5,16,17], multipliers [9,23], dividers [7,21], etc.

Among arithmetic circuits, multiplier circuits play a major role to improve the performance of data processing in a processor. Squaring is the most commonly used function in division (Newton Raphson division and Taylor series expansion), roots, or reciprocals [10,12]. Squaring also finds its applications in DSP applications such as Euclidean distance computation and exponent calculation in cryptography. For powering functions like squares and cubes, a reversible circuitry of multiplier is not the most efficient solution as it results in redundant partial products and extra addition circuitry that will result in enormous overhead in terms of quantum cost, ancilla bits, and garbage outputs. As ancilla inputs and garbage outputs are overhead bits in a reversible circuit and reversible quantum computers of many qubits are extremely difficult to realize, we propose a garbageless reversible circuit design for square computation based on recursion. Recursion technique is adapted from Karatsuba's recursive method to compute square of an operand. Inverse computation units are designed to retrieve the inputs and obtain garbageless circuit. Further, we compared proposed circuit design with existing reversible square designs and observed that our work improves number of input lines which includes data lines and ancilla lines for data width >8.

The paper is organized as follows: Sect. 2 presents the background on reversible logic gates; Sects. 3 and 4 elaborate on the design and comparative analysis of proposed reversible circuitry for square respectively; Sect. 5 presents discussion and conclusion.

2   Background on Reversible Logic Gates

The reversible gates used in this work are discussed in this section. Each reversible gate has a cost associated with it called quantum cost. The quantum cost of a

$$A \quad\oplus\quad P = \overline{A}$$

Fig. 1. NOT gate

reversible gate is the number of 1×1 and 2×2 reversible gates or quantum logic gates [14] required in designing it. The quantum cost of all reversible 1×1 and 2×2 gates is taken as unity. NOT gate shown in the Fig. 1 is an example of 1×1 reversible gate.

2.1   CNOT or Feynman Gate (FG)

CNOT gate is a 2×2 gate with inputs A and B, where A is the control line and B is the target line. The outputs have two lines; the control line directly passes A to output line while the target line passes transformed B as $B \rightarrow A \oplus B$. Figure 2 shows the block diagram and symbol of CNOT gate.

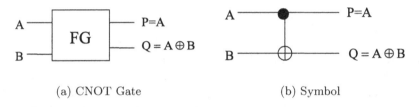

(a) CNOT Gate   (b) Symbol

Fig. 2. CNOT gate, and its quantum representation

2.2   Toffoli Gate

Figure 3 shows a Toffoli gate and its symbolic representation. It is a 3×3 gate with inputs (A, B, C) and outputs $P = A$, $Q = B$, $R = AB \oplus C$. Toffoli gate is one of the most popular reversible gates and has quantum cost of 5. The quantum cost of Toffoli gate is 5 as it needs five 2×2 quantum gates for its implementation.

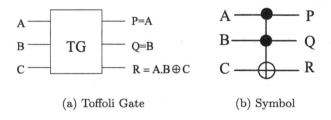

(a) Toffoli Gate   (b) Symbol

Fig. 3. Toffoli gate and its quantum representation

2.3 Peres Gate

Figure 4 shows the Peres gate and its symbolic representation. It is a 3×3 reversible gate having inputs (A, B, C) and outputs $P = A$, $Q = A \oplus B$, $R = AB \oplus C$. The quantum cost of Peres gate is 4 as it requires four 2×2 reversible gates in its design.

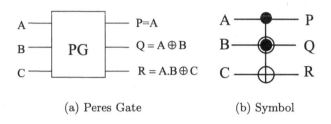

(a) Peres Gate   (b) Symbol

Fig. 4. Peres gate and its quantum representation

2.4 Reversible Full Adder (RFA)

Figure 5 shows the quantum diagram and symbol of reversible full adder [18]. It is a 4×4 reversible block. We alter the inputs given to the RFA block as $(C, B, A, 0)$ to obtain S as Carry out $(Cout)$ and R as Sum expression of reversible full adder. The quantum cost of RFA is 6 as it requires six 2×2 quantum gates. In this work, 1 bit reversible full adder is being used in the design of 3 bit reversible square circuitry (Fig. 7(b)).

3   Proposed Dedicated Reversible Square Circuit

In this work, we propose a recursive method based design of n bit square circuit. Dedicated design of square circuit is presented in [1,8] which proved to be better than the existing efficient multipliers in the literature. By applying equivalence relation, we obtained partial product reduction as shown in [8]. The motivation for the proposed design is derived from Karatsuba's algorithm [11]. We initially illustrate the method with a recursive algorithm and then proceed with the general architecture.

3.1 Recursive Square Computation Method

Let a be an n bit number. We split a into aL and aR respectively. aL represents the number coming from first $[n/2]$ bits and aR represents the second $[n/2]$ bits; therefore, we have $a = aL * 2^{n/2} + aR$. We compute square of n bit number a as:

$$a^2 = \left(aL * 2^{n/2} + aR\right)\left(aL * 2^{n/2} + aR\right)$$
$$= aL^2 * 2^n + (aL * aR + aR * aL) \, 2^{n/2} + aR^2 \qquad (1)$$

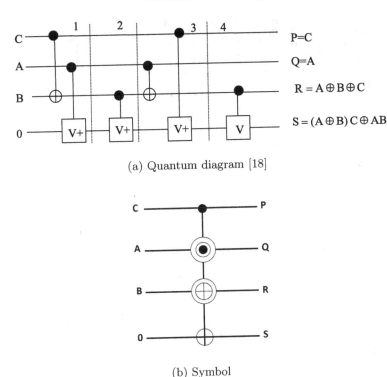

(a) Quantum diagram [18]

(b) Symbol

Fig. 5. Reversible full adder and its symbol

The second term is computed as below:

$$(aL * aR + aR * aL) = (aL + aR)(aL + aR) - (aL^2) - (aR^2) \qquad (2)$$

The squaring is done recursively using the similar kind of splitting until we arrive at a constant number of bits. We choose this constant to be 2 and 3 so that we are guaranteed that the number of bits decreases in every recursive step. At this point, we directly square the number.

1: **procedure** SQUARE(a)   ▷ compute square of a
2:     input:n bit unsigned number a
3:     output:$2n$ bit unsigned number   ▷ a^2
4:     if $a \leq 3$ then return a^2;
5:     Let aL and aR be the leftmost $\lceil n/2 \rceil$ and rightmost $\lceil n/2 \rceil$ of input a respectively
6:         $P1 \leftarrow SQUARE(aL)$;
7:         $P2 \leftarrow SQUARE(aR)$;
8:         $P_3' \leftarrow ADD(aL, aR)$;
9:         $P_3 \leftarrow SQUARE(P_3')$;
10:        return $P1 * 2^n + (P3 - (P1 + P2)) * 2^{n/2} + P2$;
11: **end procedure**

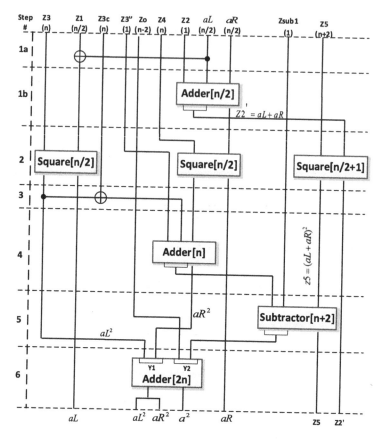

Fig. 6. Recursive square design:computation steps

3.2   Proposed Design Methodology

We present the design of dedicated square computation unit without garbage outputs. The proposed design comprises of few computational blocks for addition and subtraction which also produces zero garbage outputs [19,20]. Consider an n bit number $a[n-1{:}0] \in \{0,1\}^n$ represents a binary number. If the number of bits in a is even, then we split a into aL coming from leftmost $[n/2]$ bits and aR from rightmost $[n/2]$ bits. If the number of bits is not even, we split aL and aR into two parts each with $[n+1]/2$ and $[n-1]/2$ bits respectively and rest of the operations are modified appropriately. For the design methodology illustration, we consider n as even and proceed. Consider the n bit number a_i split into aR_i and aL_i, stored at locations AR_i where $0 \le i \le n/2 - 1$ and AL_i where $n/2 \le i \le n-1$ respectively. Further, consider that memory location z is initialized with ancilla 0 bits. Ancilla locations used in each design step vary in size and name, hence it is defined in the corresponding design step. At the end of the computation, the ancilla locations will hold a^2, while the values aL and aR are restored.

We present the design steps in two phases. Phase 1 comprises of computation steps as shown in Fig. 6 to compute square of an n bit operand. Phase 2 comprises of decomputation steps and are required to remove garbage bits.

Phase 1: Computation Steps

1. Step 1: For $0 \leq i \leq n/2 - 1$

   a: At pair of locations AL and $z1$ (here $z1$ represents ancilla 0 bits, where $z1[n/2-1:0] \in \{0\}^n$) apply $n/2$ CNOT gate array such that location AL will maintain the same value whereas $z1$ will hold the copy of aL value. The transformation of $z1$ and AL location values are shown below. Here, $*z1$ represents the value present in the location $z1$.

$$\bigotimes_{i=0}^{n/2-1} |*z1_i \oplus aL_i\rangle \, |aL_i\rangle \tag{3}$$

   This step needs $n/2$ ancilla input bits.

   b: At locations AL, AR, and $z2$, apply $n/2$ bit adder. $z2$ initially will hold ancilla 0 bit. AR will maintain the same value whereas AL transforms to s_i; $z2$ transforms to c_i state. s_i and c_i indicate the sum and carry bits generated during addition operation irrespective of the design steps. The locations $z2$ and AL are referred as $z2'$ which holds c_i bit as MSB and s_i bits as LSB bits.

$$z2' = \begin{cases} s_i & \text{for } 0 \leq i \leq n/2 - 1 \\ c_{n/2} & \text{for } i = n/2 \end{cases} \tag{4}$$

$$s_i = \begin{cases} aL_i \oplus aR_i \oplus c_i & \text{for } 0 \leq i \leq n/2 - 1 \\ c_{n/2} & \text{for } i = n/2 \end{cases} \tag{5}$$

   where c_i is the carry bit and is defined as:

$$c_i = \begin{cases} 0 & i = 0 \\ (aL_{i-1} \oplus aR_{i-1})c_{i-1} \oplus aL_{i-1}aR_{i-1} & 1 \leq i \leq n/2 \end{cases} \tag{6}$$

   This step needs 1 ancilla input bit.

   Steps 1a and 1b are executed sequentially.

2. Step 2: Apply values present at locations $z1$, AR, and $z2'$ to square computation units which operates on the operand width $n/2$, $n/2$, and $n/2+1$ respectively. Each square computation block executes recursively until operand width boils down to 3 (go to step 2 until $n = 2$ or 3). Each square computation block takes second operand as ancilla inputs stored at locations $z3$, $z4$, and $z5$ respectively, where width of $z3$, $z4$, and $z5$ are n, n, and $n + 2$ bits respectively. At the end of recursive computation $z1$, AR and $z2'$ will maintain its value as shown in Step 1a and Step 1b respectively. The ancilla

locations $z3$, $z4$, and $z5$ will hold the computation result as shown below. $*z3$, $*z4$, and $*z5$ represent the values at the locations $z3$, $z4$, and $z5$ respectively. Here, k and l indicate the bit position and n is the number of bits used to represent the operand value. The below shown equations need to be computed with $n = 2$ (for $*z3$, $*z4$), $n = 3$ (for $*z5$); these are computed when recursive call reaches $n = 2$ or 3.

$$* z3 = \bigotimes_{k=0}^{n-1} |aL_k\rangle\, 2^{2k} \oplus \bigotimes_{k=0}^{n-2} \bigotimes_{l=k+1}^{n-1} |aL_k \cdot aL_l\rangle 2^{k+l+1} \tag{7}$$

$$* z4 = \bigotimes_{k=0}^{n-1} |aR_k\rangle 2^{2k} \oplus \bigotimes_{k=0}^{n-2} \bigotimes_{l=k+1}^{n-1} |aR_k \cdot aR_l\rangle 2^{k+l+1} \tag{8}$$

$$* z5 = \bigotimes_{k=0}^{n-1} |(aL+aR)_k\rangle 2^{2k} \oplus \bigotimes_{k=0}^{n-2} \bigotimes_{l=k+1}^{n-1} |(aL+aR)_k\rangle \cdot |(aL+aR)_l\rangle 2^{k+l+1} \tag{9}$$

The square computation circuit designs for 2 bit and 3 bit square units are given in Fig. 7(a), (b). *This step needs $3n + 2$ ancilla input bits.*

3. Step 3: Apply an array of n CNOT gates at locations $(z3, z3c)$. At the end of computation, $z3$ will maintain the same value whereas $z3c$ will have the copy of $*z3$ as shown below.

$$| * z3c\rangle = \bigotimes_{i=0}^{n-1} | * z3_i\rangle \oplus | * z3c_i\rangle \tag{10}$$

$$where\ z3c\,[n-1:0]\ \in \{0\}^n$$

This step needs n ancilla input bits.

4. Step 4: Apply values present at $z3c$ and $z4$ locations to adder which adds two operands of n bit width each. To store the carry out bit, an ancilla bit location $z3''$ is given as third operand. After the computation, $z4$ will maintain the same value whereas the value at location $z3c$ will be transformed as shown below. Since output of adder is concatenated output of sum and carry bit, we need an additional ancilla zero bit, so we append one ancilla zero location($z3''$) to $z3c$ to hold the carry out bit. We refer transformed $z3c$ location as $z3''$ here onwards.

$$z3'' = \begin{cases} s_i & \text{for } 0 \le i \le n-1 \\ c_n & \text{for } i = n \end{cases} \tag{11}$$

$$s_i = \begin{cases} *z3c_i \oplus *z4_i \oplus c_i & 0 \le i \le n-1 \\ c_n & i = n \end{cases} \tag{12}$$

where c_i is the carry bit and is defined as:

$$c_i = \begin{cases} 0 & i = 0 \\ (*z3c_{i-1} \oplus *z4_{i-1})c_{i-1} \oplus *z3c_{i-1} * z4_{i-1} & 1 \le i \le n \end{cases} \tag{13}$$

This step needs 1 ancilla bit.

5. Step 5: Apply values present at locations $z5$ and $z3''$ as inputs at the subtractor unit. After the computation, $z5$ location retains its value whereas values at $z3''$ will be transformed as below. D_i indicates difference and B_i indicates borrow bits. We append an ancilla bit to location $z3''$ to adjust the width mismatch between the operands. We continue to refer $z3''$ with the same name.

$$z3'' = \begin{cases} D_i & \text{for } 0 \leq i \leq n \\ B_{n+1} & \text{for } i = n+1 \end{cases} \tag{14}$$

$$D_i = \begin{cases} *z3''_i \oplus *z5_i \oplus B_i & \text{for } 0 \leq i \leq n \\ B_{n+1} & \text{for } i = n+1 \end{cases} \tag{15}$$

where B_i is the borrow bit and is defined as:

$$B_i = \begin{cases} 0 & i = 0 \\ \overline{(*z3''_{i-1} \oplus *z5_{i-1})}B_{i-1} \oplus *z3''_{i-1} \cdot \overline{*z5_{i-1}} & 1 \leq i \leq n+1 \end{cases} \tag{16}$$

This step needs 1 ancilla bit.

6. Step 6: Apply values present at locations $(z3, z4)$ and $z3''$ to $2n$ bit wide binary adder as first and second operand respectively. Here, $*z3$ and $*z4$ are concatenated and considered as single operand. After the computation, $*z3$ and $*z4$ will maintain the same value. $z3''$ will transform to the state as shown below. Here, both the operand width are not same, so $z3''$ is appended with $n/2$ ancilla bits on its LSB side and $n/2-2$ ancilla bits on its MSB side. This extended location of $z3''$ is referred as $Y2$ and concatenated locations $(z3, z4)$ are referred as $Y1$. Now, resultant at location $Y2$ is computed as below.

$$*Y2 = \begin{cases} s_i & \text{for } 0 \leq i \leq 2n-1 \\ c_n & \text{for } i = 2n \end{cases} \tag{17}$$

$$s_i = \begin{cases} *Y1_i \oplus *Y2_i \oplus c_i & \text{for } 0 \leq i \leq 2n-1 \\ c_{2n} & \text{for } i = 2n \end{cases} \tag{18}$$

where c_i is the carry bit and is defined as:

$$c_i = \begin{cases} 0 & \text{for } i = 0 \\ (*Y1_{i-1} \oplus *Y2_{i-1})c_{i-1} \oplus *Y1_{i-1} * Y2_{i-1} & \text{for } 1 \leq i \leq 2n \end{cases} \tag{19}$$

This step needs n-2 ancilla input bits.

Phase 2: Decomputation Steps
The design steps shown here comprise of decomputation steps, which is necessary to remove the garbage bits generated in Phase 1. Design steps illustrated here are shown in Fig. 8.

7. Step 7: Apply values of locations $(z3, z1)$, $(z4, AR)$, and $(z5, z2')$ to inverse square computation blocks. The design of Inverse square blocks are same as square blocks. At the end of computation, $z1, AR$, and $z2'$ will retain the same values; $z3, z4$, and $z5$ will hold ancilla 0 bits.

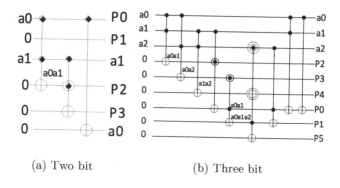

(a) Two bit   (b) Three bit

Fig. 7. Square design of two and three bits

8. Step 8: Apply values at locations AR and $z2'$ to subtractor of width $n/2+1$. At the end of computation, AR will retain the same value; $z2'$ is transformed to hold MSB $n/2$ bits of input a, so $*z2' = aL$. To adjust the width of the operands, an ancilla 0 bit is appended. This block releases two ancilla bits after the computation. *This Step requires an ancilla bit.*
9. Step 9: There are two copies of aL bits generated from Step 7 and Step 8. Apply values at locations $z1$ and $z2'$ to $n/2$ array of CNOT gates. After the computation, $z2'$ will retain aL, whereas $z1$ will hold $n/2$ ancilla 0 bits. After this step, input aL is regenerated. Thus, no garbage is produced in the computation of square. Total number of ancilla inputs required for each recursive call in this methodology is $5n + n/2 + 4$.

The complete architecture comprising of computation and decomputation steps is shown in Fig. 9.

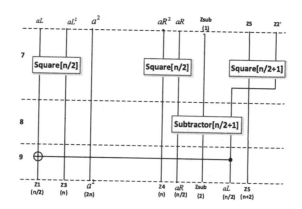

Fig. 8. Recursive square design:decomputation steps

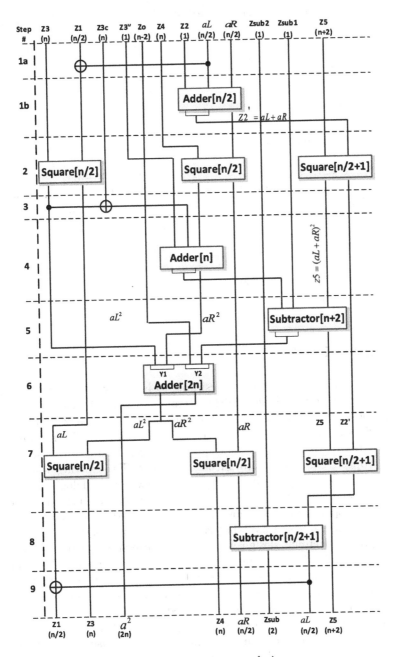

Fig. 9. Recursive square design

Table 1. Input lines comparison of reversible square designs

Data width	Proposed design	Design in-[1] Method 1	Design in-[1] Method 2	Design in-[8]
4	30	11	11	17
8	78	55	52	65
16	218	239	228	257
32	644	991	964	1025
64	1944	4031	3972	4097
128	5896	16255	16132	16385

Table 2. Input lines comparison with Karatsuba multiplier [11]

Data width	Parallel execution		Sequential execution	
n	Design in-[11]	Proposed square	Design in-[11]	Proposed square
4	44	30	44	30
8	174	114	118	78
16	596	382	308	218
32	1926	1218	830	644
64	6044	3790	2308	1944
128	18654	11634	6598	5896

4   Comparative Analysis

In reversible logic systems, it is not desirable to have garbage, so we have presented garbageless square design. In the literature, there exist dedicated square designs proposed by authors in [1,8]. Our work utilizes $(5n + n/2 + 4)$ of ancilla bits(per recursive call) and produces zero garbage outputs. These values are obtained by taking case study of adder and subtractor designs proposed in [18–20]. The proposed work has zero garbage outputs. The existing works in [8] has $n^2 - 2n + 1$ number of garbage outputs. The two methodologies in [1] have $(n^2 - 3n - 2)$ and $(n^2 - 4n - 7)$ number of garbage outputs in the first and second approach respectively. This shows that the proposed work is best optimized in terms of garbage outputs as it has zero garbage bits overhead. Further, we compared proposed circuit design with existing reversible square designs. The improvements obtained are significant compared to existing works. We observed that our work improves number of input lines which includes data lines and ancilla lines for data width >8 compared to [1,8], except the case when data width is ≤8. The comparison result is captured in Table 1.

In Table 2, we present the results of comparison with Karatsuba multiplier design [11]. The parallel execution of recursive calls make use of separate ancilla work bits, whereas sequential recursive calls reuse the ancilla bits released by previous recursive call. In both the execution methods, the improvement is seen for proposed reversible square circuit. Since the objective of this work is to optimize ancilla bits, in Table 1, we have shown ancilla bits calculation with respect to sequential recursive execution.

5 Discussion and Conclusion

In reversible computing, garbage bits and ancilla lines are considered as the design overhead. We have presented a new design of garbageless (zero garbage bits) reversible square computation circuit using recursive computation method. Further, the proposed design has improvement in terms of input lines compared to existing works in [1,8]. The algorithm is functionally verified. Virtual verification is carried out by functional simulation using Xilinx ISE simulator.

The reversible square computation unit is a key component in digital signal processor and finds application in Newton Raphson divider, Euclidean distance computation, etc. The proposed work of designing the garbageless reversible circuitry will have a tremendous contribution in designing an efficient reversible hardware.

References

1. Banerjee, A., Das, D.K.: Squaring in reversible logic using iterative structure. In: 2014 East-West Design & Test Symposium (EWDTS), pp. 1–4. IEEE (2014)
2. Bennett, C.H.: Logical reversibility of computation. IBM J. Res. Dev. **17**(6), 525–532 (1973)
3. Choi, B.S., Van Meter, R.: A $\theta(\sqrt{n})$-depth quantum adder on the 2D NTC quantum computer architecture. ACM J. Emerg. Technol. Comput. Syst. (JETC) **8**(3), 24 (2012)
4. Cuccaro, S.A., Draper, T.G., Kutin, S.A., Moulton, D.P.: A new quantum ripple-carry addition circuit. arXiv preprint quant-ph/0410184 (2004)
5. Draper, T.G., Kutin, S.A., Rains, E.M., Svore, K.M.: A logarithmic-depth quantum carry-lookahead adder. arXiv preprint quant-ph/0406142 (2004)
6. Haghparast, M., Bolhassani, A.: Optimized parity preserving quantum reversible full adder/subtractor. Int. J. Quantum Inf. **14**(03), 1650019 (2016)
7. Jamal, L., Babu, H.M., et al.: Efficient approaches to design a reversible floating point divider. In: 2013 IEEE International Symposium on Circuits and Systems (ISCAS), pp. 3004–3007. IEEE (2013)
8. Jayashree, H.V., Thapliyal, H., Agrawal, V.K.: Design of dedicated reversible quantum circuitry for square computation. In: 27th International Conference on VLSI Design and 13th International Conference on Embedded Systems, pp. 551–556. IEEE (2014)
9. Jayashree, H.V., Thapliyal, H., Arabnia, H.R., Agrawal, V.K.: Ancilla-input and garbage-output optimized design of a reversible quantum integer multiplier. J. Supercomputing **72**(4), 1477–1493 (2016)
10. Oberman, S.F., Flynn, M.: Division algorithms and implementations. IEEE Trans. Comput. **46**(8), 833–854 (1997)
11. Portugal, R., Figueiredo, C.: Reversible Karatsubas algorithm. J. Universal Comput. Sci. **12**(5), 499–511 (2006)
12. Rabinowitz, P.: Multiple-precision division. Commun. ACM **4**(2), 98 (1961)

13. Shoaei, S., Haghparast, M.: Novel designs of nanometric parity preserving reversible compressor. Quantum Inf. Process. **13**(8), 1701–1714 (2014)
14. Smolin, J.A., Di Vincenzo, D.P.: Five two-bit quantum gates are sufficient to implement the quantum Fredkin gate. Phys. Rev. A **53**(4), 2855–2856 (1996)
15. Takahashi, Y.: Quantum arithmetic circuits: a survey. IEICE Trans. Fundam. Electron. Commun. Comput. Sci. **92**(5), 1276–1283 (2009)
16. Takahashi, Y., Kunihiro, N.: A linear-size quantum circuit for addition with no ancillary qubits. Quantum Inf. Comput. **5**(6), 440–448 (2005)
17. Takahashi, Y., Kunihiro, N.: A fast quantum circuit for addition with few qubits. Quantum Inf. Comput. **8**(6), 636–649 (2008)
18. Thapliyal, H.: Mapping of subtractor and adder-subtractor circuits on reversible quantum gates. In: Gavrilova, M.L., Tan, C.J.K. (eds.) Transactions on Computational Science XXVII. LNCS, vol. 9570, pp. 10–34. Springer, Heidelberg (2016)
19. Thapliyal, H., Ranganathan, N.: Design of efficient reversible binary subtractors based on a new reversible gate. In: 2009 IEEE Computer Society Annual Symposium on VLSI, ISVLSI 2009, pp. 229–234. IEEE (2009)
20. Thapliyal, H., Ranganathan, N.: Design of efficient reversible logic-based binary and BCD adder circuits. ACM J. Emerg. Technol. Comput. Syst. (JETC) **9**(3), 17 (2013)
21. Thapliyal, H., Varun, T., Munoz-Coreas, E.: Quantum circuit design of integer division optimizing ancillary qubits and T-count. arXiv preprint arxiv:1609.01241 (2016)
22. Vedral, V., Barenco, A., Ekert, A.: Quantum networks for elementary arithmetic operations. Phys. Rev. A **54**(1), 147 (1996)
23. Moghadam, M.Z., Navi, K.: Ultra-area-efficient reversible multiplier. Microelectronics J. **43**(6), 377–385 (2012)

Methods of Registration of Weak Radio Signals

Stanislav Klimenko[1], Andrey Klimenko[2], Kira Konich[3], Igor Nikitin[4(✉)],
Lialia Nikitina[4], Valery Malofeev[5], and Sergey Tyul'bashev[5]

[1] Institute of Computing for Physics and Technology,
Moscow Institute for Physics and Technology (State University), Protvino, Russia
stanislav.klimenko@gmail.com
[2] Cyprus Space Exploration Organisation, Nicosia, Cyprus
andy.klimenko@gmail.com
[3] Bauhaus University, Weimar, Germany
kira.konycheva@uni-weimar.de
[4] Fraunhofer Institute for Algorithms and Scientific Computing,
Sankt Augustin, Germany
{igor.nikitin,lialia.nikitina}@scai.fraunhofer.de
[5] Pushchino Radio Astronomy Observatory,
Lebedev Physical Institute, Pushchino, Russia
{malofeev,serg}@prao.ru

Abstract. In this paper we will consider a problem of registration of radio signals from distant sources, natural (pulsars) or artificial (SETI signals). These signals possess a number of common properties, i.e. they are weak, almost indistinguishable from the background noise, are strongly localized on celestial sphere, have spectral characteristics smeared by dispersion on interstellar medium and Doppler drift, suffer from near-Earth electromagnetic interference. In this paper we will overview existing methods for registration of such signals and discuss some alternatives. We implement selected methods as data filters connected to data processing workflow, with 3D Virtual Environment as a frontend, integrate the methods into a system for radio astronomical monitoring *StarWatch* and apply them for detection of pulsar signals from BSA telescope at Pushchino Radio Astronomy Observatory and narrow band signals in SETI database (setilive.org).

1 Introduction

Big Scanning Antenna, BSA (also known as Large Phased Array, LPA) is a radio telescope used at Pushchino Radio Astronomy Observatory. It is a radio telescope of the meridian type with a filled aperture – a flat array of 16384 equidistant wave dipoles of a size $187\,\mathrm{m} \times 384\,\mathrm{m}$, operating at a frequency of 109–113 MHz. It is one of the most sensitive telescopes in the world in this range. BSA is used in a number of projects: in the study of pulsars, dynamic processes in near-solar and interplanetary plasma, analysis of the structure of compact radio sources, investigation of active galactic nuclei in the meter wavelength range [1–4].

Allen Telescope Array (ATA-42) is a radio telescope, located in Hat Creek, California. The telescope consists of 42 antennas in LNSD configuration, Large

© Springer-Verlag GmbH Germany 2017
M.L. Gavrilova and C.J. Kenneth Tan (Eds.): Trans. on Comput. Sci. XXIX, LNCS 10220, pp. 47–63, 2017.
DOI: 10.1007/978-3-662-54563-8_3

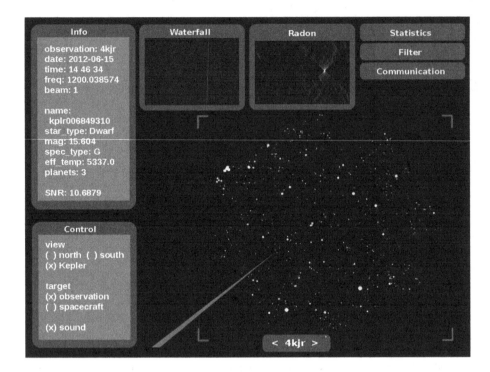

Fig. 1. StarWatch Virtual Environment. Sky map represents the observations from the database setilive.org. Several panels display the results of various data filters (Radon transform etc.) and meta-information for selected observation. Color of the ray shows signal classification: blue ray – background noise, red ray – near-Earth interference, green ray – a candidate for extraterrestrial signal. (Color figure online)

Number of Small Dishes, every of 6 m diameter. The array supports simultaneous data acquisition from several directions on celestial sphere at angular resolution approximately 4' × 2' and frequency range 0.5–11.2 GHz. The telescope is primarily used by SETI Institute in its challenging project, search for extraterrestrial intelligence.

Setilive.org is a web project forwarding SETI data for the analysis of volunteers. Till 12-Oct-2014 it supported live feeds of signals from ATA-42, which then have been discontinued. Now setilive.org serves as a large archive of radio astronomical data with more than 1.5 millions observations for more than 7.5 thousands observation targets, including directions to exoplanets discovered by telescope Kepler and other sources [5,6]. On the way of its development, SETI used various telescopes, Green Bank Telescope in West Virginia [7], Arecibo Telescope in Puerto Rico [8] and many others. Occasionally, the search brings positive detections, e.g. so called Wow!-signal, a famous registration done on 15-Aug-1977 by telescope Big Ear in Ohio [9]. The signal was located in Sagittarius constellation, close to the hydrogen line frequency, possessed very strong signal-to-noise ratio SNR $\sim$ 30, lasted 72 s and never repeated again. Recent finding is a

2 s long signal at 11 GHz, received 15-May-2015 in the direction of HD164595, a G-type star from Hercules constellation, by Russian radio observatory RATAN-600 [10]. Although several SETI telescopes were set in this direction, there were no follow-up signals registered.

Our previous paper [11] introduces a system for radio astronomical monitoring *StarWatch*. It includes a generic interface to observation databases, supports special tools for signal extraction and analysis and uses 3D Virtual Environment as a frontend (Fig. 1). Stereoscopic perception provides a convenient way for representation of multidimensional and multiscale data, produced by the telescope and data processing algorithms, as well as for interactive screening of the results. While [11] focuses on the usage of Virtual Environments, the present paper goes deeper into details of underlying methodology. Since the input data usually come in form of plain images, the software can be applied to live feeds or other signal collections possessing similar data organization. In papers [12–15] the system has been applied for analysis of signals from setilive archive and pulsar observations data from BSA.

The signals of both types come from distant sources and have a common signature. In particular, they are localized in a fixed point on celestial sphere. In addition, the signals are localized either in frequency domain (narrow band) or in time domain (sharp pulses). SETI signals are expected to be narrow band and possessing Doppler drift due to relative motion of signal source and the telescope [16,17]. Pulsar signals have a form of sharp pulses and have frequency dependent delays due to dispersion on interstellar medium [2,18]. The both effects smear the signal over the exposition time, similarly to a camera shake smearing the snapshot. The other kind of problems are created by imperfectness of radio telescope, whose directional diagram possesses so called side lobes [19–21]. As a result, signals from strong nearby sources, e.g. satellites, leak to the telescope from various directions and are mixed with the actual signal.

The present paper describes the methods helping to overcome these problems. The methods can be implemented as data filters connected to a data processing workflow, which typically consists of the following steps.

Statistical accumulation: the signals from distant sources are expected to be weaker than the background noise, with signal-to-noise ratio SNR < 1. Special filters are applied to amplify SNR and distinguish signals from the noise. There are several filters, suitable for this purpose: Radon transform [14], its varieties [22–24], autocorrelation [25], estimation of entropy and cryptographic strength of a signal [15], etc.

Selection of single beams: the measurements are performed simultaneously in several directions on celestial sphere, called beams. SETI performs precise targeting of the beams to the predefined list of objects, so that the signals from distant sources can contribute only in one beam. Meridian telescopes like BSA perform continuous scan of the sky, and the signals can appear in one or two neighbour beams. This selection allows to exclude signals from terrestrial and near-Earth sources, such as radio stations, aircrafts and satellites, which usually contribute to multiple beams [26].

Cross-validation: it happens that signals possess copies in a nearby frequency band, registered in a completely different spatial direction. All such signals must be excluded [7]. The signals from distant sources cannot move rapidly across the sky like the near-Earth sources. Also, the distant sources contribute only to the main lobe of the telescope, while strong signals from near-Earth sources penetrate through side lobes and can be registered from any direction. Rejection of such signals is a hard task, since it requires their pairwise comparison with all measurements in the database.

StarWatch Virtual Environment has been developed in Avango VE framework (avango.com), using Open Scene Graph as graphics engine, Python and C++ as API. This architecture allows rapid development of utterly complex applications, while the task of 3D visualization is overtaken by the framework, using a concept of universal display. Dependently on display configuration, StarWatch can work as a simple desktop application, with 3D capable office beamer providing resolution in megapixel range, in full immersive systems with tens megapixels resolution (PowerWalls), Large Ultra-High Resolution Displays (LUHRDs) with hundreds megapixels (CAVE2, HORNET, Stallion, hyperwall-2) or even 1.5 gigapixel (Reality Deck) [27].

In the following sections we will overview the methods for detection of weak radio signals from distant sources and demonstrate their application on narrow band signals from setilive archive and pulsar observations data from BSA telescope.

2   Statistical Accumulation

Setilive data come in form of so called waterfall plots, which represent frequency spectrum (horizontal axis) varying in time (vertical axis). Typical waterfall plots are shown on Fig. 2. Narrow band signals on these plots have a form of straight lines possessing a slope to the vertical axis due to Doppler drift.

Pulsar signals have a form of periodically repeating spikes. Being separated to several equidistant wide frequency bands, they show equidistant delays, appearing due to dispersion of the signal on interstellar medium, see Fig. 3. On the waterfall plots the spikes form similar straight lines as setilive signals, although they are produced by the other physical mechanism.

Radon transform is used for detection of straight lines on the waterfall plots. It is the integral of the form:

$$R(x, \alpha) = \int dy \, w(x \cos \alpha - y \sin \alpha, x \sin \alpha + y \cos \alpha)$$

where $w(x, y)$ is the waterfall plot and α is the slope parameter. This integral accumulates lines into points and amplifies SNR by a factor $n^{1/2}$ for the images of size $n \times n$. Radon transform is equivalent to Hough transform [28], a standard

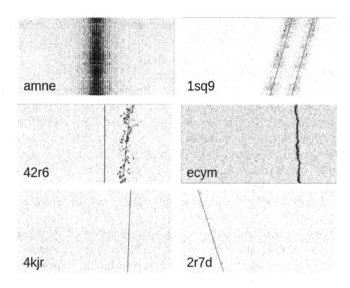

Fig. 2. Typical setilive signals. The figure shows waterfall plots – frequency spectrum (horizontal axis) varying in time (vertical axis): (amne) terrestrial source; (1sq9) GPS satellites; (42r6) combination of terrestrial and satellite signals; (ecym) satellite signal, wavy form indicates own rotation; (4kjr) single beam - potential signal of ET origination; (2r7d) one more single beam. The plots can be retrieved by their 4-character code from <talk.setilive.org/observation_groups/GSL000****>.

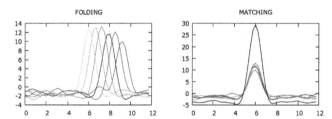

Fig. 3. Typical pulsar signal from BSA telescope: PSR J2113+2754 (B2110+27) with catalogue period P = 1.20285 s (P = 1.20293 s from search program) and catalogue dispersion measure DM = 25.1 pc/cm^3 (22.9 ± 5 pc/cm^3 from search program). On the left: the result of folding transform, the peaks in 6 frequency bands arrive at different time due to dispersion on interstellar medium; on the right: matching transform collects the peaks together and increases total SNR. The figure shows SNR as a function of time, in data points.

technique used in image processing for detection of straight lines. Direct numerical evaluation of the integral in Radon transform requires $O(n^3)$ floating point operations, while there are also faster methods, performing at $O(n^2 \log n)$ rate [22, 23].

Folding transform is used for detection of generic periodic signals. It has a form:

$$F(\phi, T) = \int dt \, s(t) \Delta(t - \phi, T)$$

where $s(t)$ is a signal, $\Delta(t, T)$ is T-periodic Dirac's function and ϕ is the phase parameter. The integral accumulates the data with equal phases from various periods and amplifies SNR for the periodic signals. The amplification factor is $(np/T)^{1/2}$, where np is the number of data points taken into analysis and T is the signal period measured in data points. The folding transform requires $O(np^2 \, log(T_1/T_0))$ operations, for the period scanned in the range $[T_0, T_1]$. Faster versions of folding transform are also known [24]. The other possibility is a computation of autocorrelator of the signal, which can be accelerated by fast Fourier transform [25].

After applying folding transform or autocorrelator in every frequency band, one needs to compensate dispersion shifts with a *matching algorithm* [15], a version of Radon transform restricted to few discrete bands. Computational complexity of direct matching algorithm is $O(np \, dpmax \, (T_1 - T_0))$, where $dpmax$ is a maximal dispersion shift, in points per frequency band. This effort is additive to the folding transform, the both should be then multiplied to the number of beams and frequency bands.

Radon and folding transforms essentially use the known form of the signal for statistical accumulation. There are also filters capable of detecting signals of unknown form. These filters are based on general statistical measures which can distinguish a given time series from a random sequence.

Entropy is generally used as a measure of chaos in a system or information content in a message. Practically it serves as a statistical measure of random uniformity of a sequence:

$$E[\rho] = \int d^n x \, f(\rho(x)), \quad f(\rho) = -\rho \log \rho$$

where $\rho(x)$ is the probability density, x is n-dimensional vector parameter, representing n sequential values of the signal. This functional achieves maximum on a uniform distribution $\rho = Const$ and can be used to measure a deviation of the probability density from the uniform distribution. The measurement should be used together with *flattening algorithm* [15], which forces every component of vector x to uniform distribution. Any signal, distorting n-dimensional joint distribution from uniform, will be detected.

Cryptographic strength. A bit sequence is called cryptographically strong, if prediction of the next bit from the previous bits of the sequence with any polynomial-time algorithm has success ratio not better than 50%. Such measure of the randomness of a given numerical sequence is evaluated by standard cryptographic tests for random number generators known as *DieHard* [29] and *DieHarder* [30]. They include a collection of subtests returning so called p-values, random variables uniformly distributed in the range $[0, 1]$ whenever the input

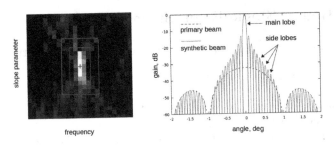

Fig. 4. On the left: selection of single beam signal on Radon plot. On the right: schematic 1D cross section of a typical beam pattern.

sequence is uniformly random. Further one performs *Kolmogorov-Smirnov test* for the uniformity of the distribution of p-values, by forming CDF of p-values and measuring its maximal deviation D_p from the linear function. Kolmogorov's distribution can be used to estimate the confidence levels, e.g. 99.73% *CL* corresponds to $D_p < 1.81 n_p^{-1/2}$, where n_p is a number of p-values.

Radon and folding transforms are known to be more sensitive for SETI and pulsar data than entropy and cryptographic filters [15], although the latter give an interesting alternative for detection of signals of unknown form.

Waterfall plots in SETI observations are typically 768×384 PNG images, rescaled to 256×256 for the purpose of our analysis. Every such observation represents 90 s scan of 533 Hz frequency band in a certain direction on celestial sphere. Processing of one observation with $O(n^3)$ method requires 0.4 s on 3 GHz Intel i7 processor. The result has a form of a bright spot on the corresponding Radon plot, see Fig. 1.

The pulsar signals from BSA telescope are registered simultaneously in a number of beams, typically $nb = 96$, and in a number of frequency bands, typically $nf = 6$ plus one cumulative. Dispersion shift is maximally $dpmax = 14$. The sampling rate is about 10 Hz, so that one minute of measurement contains $np = 600$ points and requires about 0.92 MB of disk space. There are also "high density" data with more severe characteristics.

One more specifics about BSA data is that the telescope beams are continuously sweeping across the sky and the pulsar signals appear in data during a restricted time interval, when the beam is directed precisely on the pulsar. Typically these intervals have 2–4 min duration and the search should be done with the overlapping, e.g. by taking 5 min segment and sequentially shifting it for 1 min along time axis. The overlapping additionally increases the computational effort, so that processing of BSA data with current methods requires in average 18 s per a minute of measurements.

Mass processing of SETI and pulsar data can be trivially parallelized to make use of all available cores and processors, so that the processing speed can be significantly increased on parallel architectures.

3   Selection of Single Beam Signals

The input waterfall plots in setilive database come in groups, corresponding to simultaneous signal observations in several directions on celestial sphere. Further we will use the following terminology:

- *observations* are all available waterfall plots in the database, including those where only noise was registered;
- *observation group* combines waterfall plots made for the same frequency at the same time, but in different spatial directions, called *beams*;
- *signals* are any events where the output of statistical accumulation filter exceeds the threshold.

Single beam signals are signals present in one beam and absent in the other beams, in the same observation group.

In our paper [12] we performed single beam selection for 1.5 millions of observations in setilive database. At first, only 3-beam observations have been selected, reducing the total number of observation groups from 673 thousands to 253 thousands. Then the signals with small Doppler drift were eliminated. Such signals are produced by the sources which don't move (or have a constant radial speed) relative to the receiver and most probably correspond to terrestrial radio sources or geostationary satellites. These signals are represented as vertical lines on waterfall plots, i.e. as nearly zero angles on Radon plots and can be easily eliminated.

Further, the signals were selected on Radon plots using a method shown on Fig. 4 left. Two rectangular contours around a given point were defined. The point is selected if a logical AND of the following conditions took place:

- in the given beam in the given point $SNR_0 > 4$;
- in the given beam everywhere between two contours $SNR < SNR_0/2$;
- in the other two beams everywhere inside external contour $SNR < 4$.

This allows to select narrow signals appearing in a single beam. Full list can be found in [12], the strongest 28 signals are given in the first column of Table 1 below. The observation can be retrieved from setilive server, by substituting 4-character observation ID to the address talk.setilive.org/observation_groups/GSL000****.

4   Cross-Validation of Single Beam Signals

Now the list of 28 strongest signals will be subjected to additional selection procedure, analogous to SETI analysis [7]. This procedure enforces single beam selection, by comparing the signals from the list pairwise with all other observations in the database. The purpose is to find similar signals in a nearby frequency band that have been recorded in directions other than the signals from the list. Radio signals from extraterrestrial sources are so weak, that their registration is only possible with precise direction of the telescope to the source. Registration of similar signals in different spatial directions excludes their extraterrestrial origin.

One evident reason why near-Earth signals are registered in different directions is a motion of the source on a sky, i.e. an aircraft or satellite. The other reason is more sophisticated.

A beam of radio telescope is really not a straight line towards a point on celestial sphere, but has a complex internal structure. Typical beam pattern is shown in 1D cross-section on Fig. 4 right. There is a two-level structure, the largest one (primary beam) is related with sensitivity diagram of one antenna dish, the smallest one (synthetic beam) – with arrangement of antennas in phased array. There is one sharp maximum (main lobe). It is the actual telescope direction that was earlier referred simply as a beam. When the phases between the elements in the phased array are changed, the main lobe moves across the sky. The other possibility is to consider several combinations of phases at a time and to scan the sky in several directions simultaneously. In this way observation groups consisting of several beams are formed.

In addition to the main lobe, there is a large number of secondary maxima (side lobes), covering a large area in the sky. Figure 4 has logarithmic scale and the gain in the side lobes is significantly smaller than the gain in the main lobe. However, the near-Earth interferers are so strong, that their side lobe contributions compete with the main lobe contributions of weak signals.

ATA-42 telescope has an angular resolution about $1°$ for a primary beam and $0.068°$ for synthetic beams [19, 20]. Radio interference enters the telescope through the side lobes, where the gain of antenna varies chaotically on the angular sizes of the order of the synthetic beam width. There is also a formfactor of the antenna, with a typical variation size of the order of the primary beam width. For any given direction of the telescope a signal from the satellite may come aside, penetrate the side lobe and mix with the main signal.

Selection of single beam signals significantly improves the situation, since the absence of a signal in several beams indicates the absence of radio interference that would penetrate through the side lobes in all beams. Continuous absence of a signal in several beams for 90 s observation is even stronger evidence, since the motion of the source of interference on the sky would result in its movement over the structure of side lobes and the signal would be inevitably registered in all beams. Only in the exceptional case, if the source of radio interference is in zero zone between the side lobes for two beams and in non-zero zone for the third beam, and such configuration persists during 90 s, the signal from the satellite will be interpreted as a single beam signal. Rejection of such signals is the purpose of cross-validation.

In particular, the cross-validation procedure in [7] uses ±1 MHz band around the tested signal for searching similar signals. As a criterion of signal similarity it is proposed to compare the bandwidth, Doppler drift and modulation type. In our work, we identify narrow band signals, most of which do not have a noticeable modulation, with a few exceptions. Such signals have the form of straight lines on waterfall plots and all look alike. Therefore, we have used the following additional selection criteria.

First of all, we pass all the observations from the database through the same statistical accumulation filter as in the search of single beam signals. This leaves only narrow bandwidth signals for further similarity tests. Selections for 3-beam observations, Doppler drift, single beams have been deactivated. Thus, in cross-validation we consider also the signals appearing in multiple beams, observation groups possessing one or two beams and signals without Doppler drift. If such signals appear in ± 1 MHz band around the tested signal, in a different spatial direction, the tested signal is rejected and the cluster of similar signals is saved for further analysis.

The purpose of this analysis is understanding the nature of the interferers contributing to single beam observations. In this paper we will test a hypothesis that the registered signal is produced by a satellite on a circular orbit of a certain height. Thus we have restrictions on the speed and acceleration resulting in restrictions on the amplitude of Doppler shift and its rate (Doppler drift):

$$\Delta f/f_0 = v_r/c, \quad f'/f_0 = a_r/c, \quad v_r = |r|', \quad a_r = |r|'',$$

where v_r, a_r are radial velocity and acceleration of the satellite relative to the telescope, $|r|$ is a distance between the satellite and the telescope, c is a speed of light, Δf, f' are Doppler shift and Doppler drift, f_0 is emitted frequency of the signal. Note that emitted frequency is unknown, however the measured frequency of the tested signal as well as all possible samples of the same signal belong to its $\pm \Delta f$ band. As an upper estimation, one can take the measured frequency as a reference and double Δf in this formula.

If the tested signal exceeds the limit on Doppler drift, the possibility of its location on the considered orbit is eliminated immediately. Otherwise all signals from similarity cluster, satisfying these constraints, are considered as potential samples of the same signal. The presence of such signals confirms the hypothesis that the tested signal is produced by a satellite on the given orbit.

The orbits of satellites are usually divided in the following categories, according to the height above the surface of Earth:

- low Earth orbits (LEO): 160–2000 km;
- medium Earth orbits (MEO): 2000–35786 km;
- geosynchronous orbits (GSO): 35786 km;
- high orbits: more than 35786 km.

GSO is a distinguished family of the orbits with a period of 24 h. This family contains a single geostationary orbit (GEO), passing along the equator, where not only the period, but also the direction of rotation of the satellite coincides with the Earth's rotation, therefore geostationary satellites are fixed relative to the surface of the Earth. Note that location of tested signal on GEO is excluded by Doppler drift selection.

For our purposes a different subdivision is suitable:

- zone I, <20 thous.km;
- zone II, 20–130 thous.km;
- zone III, >130 thous.km.

This subdivision is related with the beam structure of ATA-42 telescope. LEO and most of MEO satellites as well as aircrafts move on celestial sphere so fast, that during the observation period they cross a number of side lobes along their way. Therefore, it is highly unlikely that signals from these objects would be registered as single beam ones. Starting from the height of 20 thous.km satellites during 90 s observation pass less than $1°$ relative to the fixed stars. Thus, it is possible that the satellite gets accidentally in the gap between the side lobes, appearing due to the formfactor of the antenna, and remains therein during the observation. Here the most probable zone for satellites which can contribute to single beam signals is located. This zone starts at MEO altitudes, covers GSO ones and ends in high orbits. At altitudes higher than 130 thous.km satellites during 90 s observation pass less than $0.068°$, here they may fall into the gap between the side lobes at the level of the synthetic beam. On the other hand, it is already a third of the Moon-Earth distance and so high orbits are also improbable.

Table 1 presents all three cases. Preference is given to the zone II, in the absence of observations there it is subjected to detailed analysis involving the neighbour zones. Figure 5 shows the distribution of observations and signals over time and frequency. In fact, this is an extension of waterfall plots discussed earlier. Every waterfall plot has a size $533\,Hz \times 90\,s$ and on Fig. 5 would occupy a tiny cell. At the same time, every plot on Fig. 5 is only a $\pm 1\,MHz$ portion of total 10 GHz search range, in addition there is a 2-dimensional space of celestial coordinates. This gives an idea of the true scale of the search. Figure 5 also shows selection zones, where the widest one corresponds to smaller heights, central one - to the medium heights, while the innermost one - to the large heights. Note that the zones are nested and all observations contained in the interior zones are also present in outer zones. Therefore, the sum of signal numbers over the height zones in Table 1 sometimes exceeds the total number of signals. A dash in place of a number in Table 1 indicates that already the original observation has violated the limit on the rate of the Doppler drift, so the signal can be excluded from this zone.

5   Discussion

For most of single beam signals in 1 MHz vicinity there is a number of signals registered in other spatial directions, many of them are located within the central zone of the extended waterfall plot. This means that the hypothesis of assignment of the given signal to a group of satellites in the middle zone of heights has an experimental confirmation. Examples shown in Table 1 allow to verify visually the availability and similarity of the signals on setilive server.

Several signals require special consideration. A group of observations 4xpv, 4xq3, 4xq5 shown on Fig. 6 is made on the same triple of targets HIP142, TYC4026-00011-1, TYC4026-00065-1. At first, the observation 4xpv is taken, then in 13 min the observations 4xq3, 4xq5 are made. The observations 4xq3, 4xq5 are made simultaneously at different frequencies, shifted from 4xpv by 55 kHz and -15 kHz respectively. In the first beam of each of these observations there are several single beam signals, two for 4xq3, two for 4xq5 and whole eight for 4xpv. Since 4xq3,

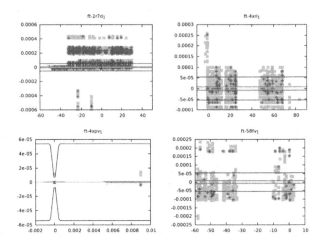

Fig. 5. Extended waterfall plots. The title of each graph is the observation ID. The horizontal axis - time in days, the vertical axis - the relative frequency deviation from the central observation. The blue dots show the observations, red dots - signals. The lines mark the limits of the Doppler shift for satellites on different heights, 0.16 thous.km blue, 20 thous.km green, 130 thous.km yellow. (Color figure online)

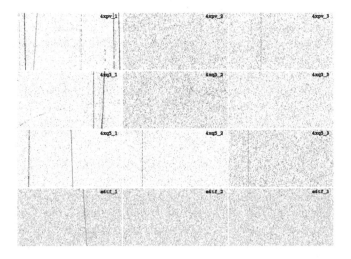

Fig. 6. Signals passed cross-validation. In each row the first waterfall plot represents several single beam signals from which the signals possessing the largest Doppler drift are marked by green. The following two plots show the next beams of the same observation. Some of them have weak signals with nearly zero Doppler drift, they are marked by the dashed green line. The interaction of these signals with the inspected ones is discussed in the text in detail. Except of these dashed signals, there are no other narrowband signals in the 1 MHz vicinity of the inspected signals. (Color figure online)

Table 1. Cross-validation

Observation obs	In ±1 MHz vicinity of obs, in directions, different from obs					
	Observations	Signals	Signals on a height (thousands of km)			Examples of signals, similar to obs
			0.16–20	20–130	>130	
1y6e_3	73411	4354	1766	499	106	0th6_*, 13k6_*, 134w_2
2r7d_1	73518	4357	1679	637	-	065r_2, 02ei_1, 03r2_*
30z4_1	73504	4358	1746	909	-	065r_2, 02ei_1, 03r2_*
3xfa_2	17640	5142	4435	1119	-	3ur3_2, 3wbj_2, 3zga_3
4bag_2	19698	2219	81	35	12	422c_*, 4235_*, 4591_*
4kjr_1	17616	5150	3781	1155	255	3thq_*, 3tii_*, 3tw8_*
4pux_2	6278	670	571	438	-	48aw_1, 48az_2, 49sz_*
4uq1_3	17660	5157	3974	1324	872	3thq_*, 3tii_*, 3tw8_*
4va8_2	17723	5170	65	11	-	4tca_*, 4tky_*, 4u4u_*
4w6w_3	19251	2198	1908	222	133	4284_1, 42f0_1, 42w8_*
4xhd_3	17667	5161	4167	790	102	3thp_*, 3tw8_*, 3u6k_1
4xpv_1	10	1	1	0	0	
4xq3_1	10	2	1	0	0	
4xq5_1	10	1	1	0	0	
4xrh_1	4706	241	195	56	31	514w_*, 52zi_*, 5682_*
4xri_1	4706	241	195	56	31	514w_*, 52zi_*, 5682_*
56ri_2	16128	621	347	178	111	4y13_2, 50xd_*, 517h_*
580l_1	741	42	39	9	2	4ypj_1, 53h2_*, 59b2_2
580w_1	741	42	31	10	4	4ypi_1, 51dl_3, 57my_1
5812_1	741	42	38	5	2	53h4_1, 50xf_*, 53h2_*
58fv_1	2153	74	13	0	0	50yi_*, 5382_3, 559r_*
e5fe_2	574	296	276	39	21	e56a_*, e56o_*, e57g_*
e6pa_1	508	3	1	1	1	e6wa_1
e6tf_1	171	0	0	0	0	
ed55_1	6277	666	38	1	1	edr4_1
ed58_1	6283	666	49	9	6	ecr3_*, ect7_*, ecwc_*
ed9f_1	10730	3844	102	31	3	3thw_*, 3tmh_*, 3tvr_*
ee5l_1	6276	669	43	2	-	edc0_2, edwe_2

4xq5 are taken simultaneously at different frequencies, they cannot contain the same signal, but they can be different frequency components of the same signal. In the next beams of observations 4xpv, 4xq5 there are weak signals with nearly zero Doppler drift, whose position on waterfall plot does not coincide with any of the signals from the first beam, that is why the latter are single beam ones. In principle, 4xpv_3 can coincide with 4xq3_1 or 4xq5_1, but not with both. Also, 4xq5_2,3 can coincide with one of the signals of 4xpv_1, but not with all eight ones. In general, 1 MHz vicinity of these observations has a total of 10 observations, which contain only two signals in a direction different from HIP142, namely the aforementioned 4xpv_3 and 4xq5_2,3. Given the complex structure of single beam signals in this triple of observations and insufficient statistics in 1 MHz vicinity, we can not confidently exclude these signals from the original list of candidates, on the basis of available data. More complete data, which other research groups may possess, will allow to continue the analysis. Table 2 shows the necessary signal parameters.

Table 2. Signals passed cross-validation

Observation	Object	Galactic coordinates (latitude, longitude)	Frequency (MHz)	Registration time (UTC)
4xpv	HIP142	66.30599976, 179.54624939	3883.268311	Thu Aug 9, 2012 18:23:38
4xq3			3883.323730	Thu Aug 9, 2012 18:36:32
4xq5			3883.252686	Thu Aug 9, 2012 18:36:32
e6tf	HIP58924	76.76242065, −1.24818373	2170.053955	Sat Sep 6, 2014 20:09:10

Observation e6tf_1 contains a single beam signal, shown on Fig. 6 bottom. In its 1 MHz vicinity there are 171 observations, which do not possess any signal except e6tf_1. Therefore, this signal passes cross-validation and its parameters are also given in Table 2.

6   Conclusion

We have described the methods for registration of weak radio signals from distant sources, tuned to the signals of the special signature:

- narrow band (SETI signals), sharp pulses (pulsar signals);
- spectral characteristics possessing Doppler drift and/or dispersion on interstellar medium;
- signal sources strongly localized on celestial sphere.

The methods suppress electromagnetic interference, in particular, they reject signals from near-Earth interferers penetrating the radio telescope through the side lobes. We have implemented the methods as data filters for statistical accumulation, selection of single beams and cross-validation. The filters are connected to data processing workflow, with 3D Virtual Environment as a frontend, integrated into a system for radio astronomical monitoring *StarWatch* and applied for detection of narrow band signals in SETI database (setilive.org) and pulsar signals from BSA telescope at Pushchino Radio Astronomy Observatory.

In analysis of setilive database, from 1.5 millions of available observations we have selected 28 signals with the signature described above. Further, 24 of them can be identified as satellite radio interference. The remaining 4 signals do not have signals of similar shape in their 1 MHz vicinity in other spatial directions. Although these 4 signals formally satisfy SETI criteria for extraterrestrial signals [7], the density of observations in the vicinity of these 4 signals is low comparing with other search areas. Unique classification of these signals requires more data in the specified direction, frequency range and time frame. Necessary signal parameters are given in Table 2.

The analysis of pulsar data from Pushchino Radio Astronomy Observatory is now running in test phase. With our implementation of folding and matching algorithms the data from 1 h measurement have been processed. All pulsars known to be present in the data at the level SNR > 5 have been extracted. Also one pulsar at the level SNR $\sim$ 3 has been found, which has not been detected in these data by previously used methods.

Our plans include further development of StarWatch Virtual Environment frontend towards Large Ultra-High Resolution Displays (LUHRDs).

When studying electromagnetic interference, detailed structure of side lobes becomes important. In our recent paper [31] we have performed visualization of wave patterns from ATA-42 telescope and have shown a presence of long valleys where satellite signals can hide. On the other hand, in this paper we have considered a far zone of the telescope, >100 km. There is also a near zone, where the beams are not formed yet and the wave pattern can possess even more complicated structure in 3 dimensions. Testing an alternative hypothesis that single beam signals are generated by an aircraft located in near zone of the telescope an interesting topic for further investigation. The above aspects are important both for the development of telescopes and the design of their serving algorithms.

Further development of highly sensitive algorithms for detection of weak radio signals is necessary in view of increasing capacity of the telescopes, used in the modern large scale astronomical projects. I.e., if the detailed information about signal phases becomes available, it allows to reconstruct signal direction with the method of aperture synthesis [32]. Improvements on the hardware side are also planned, here we mention increasing the number of dishes in SETI ATA telescope (ATA-350), linking multiple on-Earth radio telescopes for creation of a virtual Earth-size telescope [33], connecting satellite and on-Earth telescopes for building interferometer with a super long Earth-orbit baseline [18]. Such powerful instruments will considerably increase the resolution and sensitivity, necessary for the search of extraterrestrial intelligence and pulsar signals, and will open new possibilities for other challenging projects.

References

1. Malofeev, V.M.: Measurements of the pulse energy of weak pulsars at frequencies of 61 and 102 MHz. Astron. Lett. **19**, 138–142 (1993)
2. Malofeev, V.M., Malov, O.I.: Detection of Geminga as a radiopulsar. Nature **389**, 697–699 (1997)
3. Chashei, I.V., et al.: Global structure of the turbulent solar wind during 24 solar activity maxima from IPS observations with the multibeam radio telescope BSA LPI at 111 MHz. Solar Phys. **290**, 2577–2587 (2015)

4. Tyul'bashev, S.A.: A study of radio sources using interplanetary scintillations at 111 MHz. Core-dominated sources. Astron. Rep. **53**, 19–29 (2009)
5. Turnbull, M.C., Tarter, J.C.: Target selection for SETI: 1. A catalog of nearby habitable stellar systems. Astrophys. J. Suppl. Ser. **145**, 181–198 (2003)
6. Turnbull, M.C., Tarter, J.C.: Target selection for SETI. II. Tycho-2 Dwarfs, old open clusters, and the nearest 100 stars. Astrophys. J. Suppl. Ser. **149**, 423–436 (2003)
7. Siemion, A.P.V., et al.: A 1.1 to 1.9 GHz SETI survey of the Kepler field: I. A search for narrow-band emission from select targets. Astrophys. J. **767**, 94–107 (2013)
8. Steele, B.: It's the 25th anniversary of Earth's first (and only) attempt to phone ET, Cornell News, 12 November 1999
9. Ehman, J.B.: The Big Ear Wow!-Signal: What We Know and Don't Know About It After 20 Years, Big Ear Radio Observatory (1997). www.bigear.org/wow20th.htm
10. Shostak, S.: SETI detects possible signal at 11 GHz frequency from sun-like star (2016). phys.org/news/2016-08-seti-ghz-frequency-sun-like-star.html
11. Klimenko, S.V., Nikitin, I.N., Malofeev, V.M.: StarWatch: radio astronomical monitoring in virtual environment. In: Proceedings of CyberWorlds 2015, Gotland, Sweden, pp. 361–364. IEEE (2015)
12. Nikitin, I.N.: Statistical analysis of narrow-band signals at setilive.org (2015). arxiv.org/abs/1502.04887
13. Klimenko, S.V., et al.: On signals with Doppler drift, fast Fourier transform and search for extraterrestrial intelligence. In: Proceedings of SCVRT 2013, Protvino, Russia, 26–28 November 2013
14. Klimenko, S.V., Nikitin, I.N.: On statistical data accumulation, Radon transform and search for extraterrestrial intelligence. In: Proceedings of CPT 2014, Cyprus, Larnaca, 11–18 May 2014
15. Konich, K., et al.: Radio astronomical monitoring in virtual environment. Procedia Comput. Sci. **66**, 592–601 (2015)
16. Osgood, D., Ekers, R.D.: SETI 2020: A Roadmap for the Search for Extraterrestrial Intelligence. SETI Press, Mountain View (2002)
17. Siemion, A.P.V., et al.: Searching for extraterrestrial intelligence with the square kilometre array. In: Proceedings of Science, AASKA14, p. 116 (2015). arxiv.org/abs/1412.4867
18. Kardashev, N.S., et al.: Review of scientific topics for the Millimetron space observatory. Physics-Uspekhi **57**, 1199–1229 (2014)
19. Welch, J., et al.: The Allen Telescope Array: the first widefield, panchromatic, snapshot radio camera for radio astronomy and SETI. Proc. IEEE **97**(8), 1438–1447 (2009). arxiv.org/abs/0904.0762
20. Harp, G.R.: Using multiple beams to distinguish radio frequency interference from SETI signals. Radio Sci. **40**, RS5S10 (2005). arxiv.org/abs/1309.3826
21. Harp, G.R., Wright, M.C.H.: Simulations of Primary Beam Sidelobe Confusion with the ATA Primary Beam, MEMO 74, SETI Institute, March 2007
22. Cullers, D.K., Deans, S.R. (eds.) SETI Algorithms, Chap. 4, The DADD (Doubling Accumulation Drift Detection) algorithm, SETI Institute (1989). ftp://ftp.seti.org/gharp/SetiAlgorithms-CullersDeans.pdf
23. Chandra, S.: Finite Transform Library (FTL), Version 1.50 (2013). finitetransform.sourceforge.net
24. Staelin, D.H.: Fast folding algorithm for detection of periodic pulse trains. Proc. IEEE **57**, 724 (1969)
25. Harp, G.R., et al.: A new class of SETI beacons that contain information. In: Communication with Extraterrestrial Intelligence. State University of New York Press (2011). arxiv.org/abs/1211.6470

26. Tutorials, S.: Signal Processing and SETI setiquest.org/about/tutorials, The Doppler Effect setilive.org/about, How would we know that the signal is from ET? www.seti.org/faq, SETI Institute 2011–2015

27. Hinkenjann, A., et al.: Large, ultra high resolution displays - LUHRDs. IEEE Virtual Reality (IEEE VR), March 2015. Tutorial. sites.google.com/site/luhrdtutorial

28. Duda, R.O., Hart, P.E.: Use of the hough transformation to detect lines and curves in pictures. Comm. ACM **15**, 11–15 (1972)

29. Marsaglia, G.: The Marsaglia Random Number CDROM Including the Diehard Battery of Tests of Randomness. Florida State University (1995). stat.fsu.edu/pub/diehard

30. Brown, R.G., Eddelbuettel, D., Bauer, D.: Dieharder: A Random Number Test Suite Version 3.31.1 (2004). www.phy.duke.edu/~rgb/General/dieharder.php

31. Klimenko, S.V., et al.: StarWatch 2.0: RFI filter for SETI signals. In: Proceedings of CyberWorlds 2016, Chongqing, China (accepted)

32. Rampadarath, H., et al.: The first very long baseline interferometric SETI experiment. Astron. J. **144**, 38 (2012)

33. ALMA Links with Other Observatories to Create Earth-size Telescope, ALMA Observatory (2015). www.almaobservatory.org

A Novel Multiple Antennas Based Centralized Spectrum Sensing Technique

Jyotshana Kanti[1]([⊠]), Geetam Singh Tomar[2,3], and Ashish Bagwari[4]

[1] Department of Computer Science and Engineering,
Uttarakhand Technical University, Dehradun, India
jyotshanakanti@gmail.com
[2] T.H.D.C.I.H.E.T., Tehri, Uttarakhand, India
gstomar@ieee.org
[3] Machine Intelligence Research Labs, Gwalior, India
[4] Department of Electronics and Communication Engineering,
Uttarakhand Technical University, Dehradun, India
ashishbagwari@ieee.org

Abstract. In wireless communication, sensing failure, reliability, and fading affects the radio signals. Adaptive threshold and multiple antennas are one of the solutions of such problems. In this paper, authors introduced a novel multiple antennas based centralized spectrum sensing (SS) technique for cognitive radio networks (CRNs). This paper is divided into two parts: part *A* uses multiple antennas based improved sensing detector (MA_ISD), and part *B* uses multiple antennas based centralized spectrum sensing (MA_CSS) technique. Now, in the part *A*: the presented scheme uses two detectors (TD) concept, first one is an energy detector with a single adaptive threshold (ED-SAT) and the second one is an energy detector with two adaptive thresholds (ED-TAT). Both detectors imply multiple antennas, following selection combination to select best signals. The proposed model enhances the detection performance and takes less sensing or detection time. The thresholds are adaptive as they are dependent on noise variance (σ_ω^2), and the value of this noise variance changes according to the noise signal. Both the detectors work simultaneously and their output is then fed to a decision device which takes the decision using an *OR* rule. Results confirm that the presented multiple antennas based improved sensing detector (MA_ISD) technique improves the detection performance by 24.6%, 53.4%, 37.9%, and 49.6%, as compared to existing schemes (i.e. EDT-ASS-2015 scheme, ED and cyclo-2010, adaptive SS-2012, and conventional-ED) scheme at -12 dB signal-to-noise ratio (SNR), respectively, while the number of antennas (N_r) = 2. Meanwhile, proposed technique also decreases sensing time in the order of 47.0 ms, 49.0 ms, and 53.2 ms as compared to existing schemes (EDT-ASS-2015, Adaptive SS-2012, and ED and Cyclo-2010) scheme at -20 dB SNR respectively. Further, in the part *B*: cooperative SS (CSS) is introduced in which the local decisions from each cognitive radio are transferred to a fusion center (FC) that decides the final decision and shares the decision to every cognitive radio. It is also found that the proposed detection technique with CSS when a number of cognitive radio (CR) users (k) = 10, and N_r = 2, achieves detection performance as per IEEE 802.22 at very low SNR i.e. -20 dB.

© Springer-Verlag GmbH Germany 2017
M.L. Gavrilova and C.J. Kenneth Tan (Eds.): Trans. on Comput. Sci. XXIX, LNCS 10220, pp. 64–85, 2017.
DOI: 10.1007/978-3-662-54563-8_4

Keywords: Cognitive radio networks · Single adaptive threshold · Two adaptive thresholds · Two detectors · Centralized spectrum sensing

1 Introduction

Nowadays, call drop is one of the major issues in wireless communication system. This happens due to the limited bandwidth, phenomena are known as "spectrum scarcity". Only the licensed users (those who have assigned or allotted frequency band) do not affect from this. But the other unlicensed users or secondary users (SUs) face spectrum scarcity problem. To resolve such problem, Federal Communication Commission (FCC) analyzed this matter and concluded in their report that this problem arises due to the shortage of spectrum because numbers of users are increasing. Therefore, the solution is to choose another appropriate frequency band whose operational characteristics are similar to the mobile band. TV band is quite similar and 70% of TV band is unused, thus efficient utilization of TV band by mobile users reduce spectrum scarcity problem [1].

Further, in 1998, Dr. Joseph Mitola proposed 5G concepts to solve the spectrum underutilization problem. In 5G or cognitive radio networks, unlicensed users utilize PU frequency bands opportunistically and efficiently when PUs do not use the same.

There are four basic functions of CRN systems, spectrum sensing, spectrum sharing, spectrum mobility, and spectrum decision [2]. Spectrum sensing defines when the SU detects available vacant bands of PUs. Therefore, various sensing techniques have been introduced by researchers to sense licensed signal. Among all detectors, conventional-ED is one who is usually used due to its ease to implement and less complexity. But its performance degrades under low SNR values.

To improve detector performance at low SNR in [3] authors introduced two-stage detectors, energy detector in the first stage and the second stage is a cyclostationary detector. But detector has limitations, computationally more complex and required longer sensing time. Moreover, to minimize sensing time, in [4], authors presented adaptive spectrum sensing scheme, in which out of two stages only one stage's detector perform sensing operation at a time. However, authors minimized sensing time but system complexity was there. Furthermore, in [5], authors presented adaptive sensing technique using energy detector (EDT-ASS). Here, authors discussed on cost-function and concluded about the primary user's (PU's) absence or presence.

In this paper, we optimize detection performance using multiple antennas with two detectors, two detectors ED_SAT and ED_TAT perform sensing operation simultaneously. Thresholds are adaptive that's why chances of occurring sensing failure problem is negligible [6]. The output results of detectors go to decision device (DD) who takes final decision using *OR*-rule, if the output of DD is 1 shows frequency band is busy (H_1), otherwise free (H_0). The main difference between this paper and others [3, 4, & 5] are that none of these techniques focused on spectrum sensing failure [6], and fading problem. Adaptive threshold scheme reduces sensing failure problem while multiple antennas mitigate the fading problem.

We further propose CSS with multiple antennas based improved sensing detector (MA_ISD). In CSS, each CR user sends local decision (0 or 1 bit) to a common centralized node known as fusion center (FC). FC uses hard decision *OR-rule* to take a final decision. Hard decision method requires less bandwidth of the control channel this is the main advantage of hard decision method [7, 8]. *OR-rule* states that if any one of the decisions of CRs outcome with 1 bit then FC's final decision indicates H_1, and viçe-versa if there are all 0 bits.

Meanwhile, [9, 10] says that the use of multiple antennas enhances the reliability of spectrum sensing in CRN.

The novelty of this paper that it deals with three issues of CRNs: reliability, sensing failure, and fading affect. The proposed model is using multiple antennas with adaptive thresholds to improve reliability & mitigate sensing failure problem, and cooperative sensing is useful to mitigate sensing failure problem. Simulation results confirm that the proposed model enhances detection performance at false alarm probability (P_f) is 0.1, performs well at low SNRs, and reduces sensing time as well.

The rest of the paper is arranged as follows: Sect. 2 discusses system description. Section 3 presents proposed system model. Section 4 presents the simulation results and analysis. Finally, Sect. 5 concludes the simulation results.

2   System Description

In CRN, CR users detect PU licensed signal, to detect primary user signal there is hypothesis test. Hypothesis test is two types, H_1 (alternate hypothesis) states that PU signal is considered as present under noisy channel, channel is additive white gaussian noise (AWGN) with zero mean, denoted as $\omega(n), \sigma_\omega^2$ denotes noise variance and received signal $r(n)$ can be defined as [2]

$$r(n) = x(n) \times h(n) + \omega(n), \quad H_1 \tag{1}$$

H_0 (null hypothesis) states that PU signal is considered as absent and received signal $r(n)$ can be defined as

$$r(n) = \omega(n), \quad H_0 \tag{2}$$

In Eqs. (1) and (2), $r(n)$ is signal sensed by CR users. $x(n)$ is primary users signal, $\omega(n)$ is additive white gaussian noise having zero mean, $h(n)$ is the gain of the channel, and n is numbers of samples i.e. $n = 1, 2, \ldots\ldots N$. Equations (1) and (2) can also be defined as: suppose Eq. (1) exists it shows that CR users cannot use PU band because of presence of PU signal and if Eq. (2) exist then CR users can use PU signal due to the absence of PU signal.

3   Proposed System Model

3.1   Multiple Antennas Based Improved Sensing Detector (MA_ISD)

Figure 1, depicts the proposed sensing model of novel multiple antennas based improved sensing detector (MA_ISD). We assume that there are N_r numbers of antennas, receiving N number of samples, and CR uses the selection combiner (SC) scheme that provides maximum SNR value signal out of N_r decision statistics. Therefore, the received signal $r = max\ (r_1, r_2, r_3, ..., r_{Nr})$ passes to upper stream and lower stream. In Fig. 1, upper stream carries ED with a single adaptive threshold, this detector is similar as conventional-ED, except adaptive threshold that's why detector is an advanced version of conventional-ED. ED with a single adaptive threshold calculates observed energy (E) of received signal $r(n)$ [2] and compares with the adaptive threshold (λ_1), then generates output (L_1) and passes to decision device (DD) in the form of binary bits. Suppose, the calculated observed energy (E) is greater than and equal to the adaptive threshold (λ_1), then the output of detector (L_1) is bit 1 else bit 0. Similarly, the lower stream carries ED with two adaptive thresholds (ED_TAT), this detector is different from the upper stream detector because it has two adaptive thresholds. Two adaptive thresholds concept is fruitful to reduce sensing failure problem [6]. Now, ED_TAT computes the energy, compares with thresholds (γ) and produces output (L_2). Suppose, the computed energy is greater and equal to γ, then the output L_2 will be bit 1 else bit 0. The outputs of detectors (ED_SAT and ED_TAT) go to decision device (DD), further, DD adds L_1 & L_2 using OR-rule operation. According to OR-rule, if the sum of L_1 & L_2 is greater or equal to 1, shows H_1 (the channel is busy), else shows H_0 (the channel is free) as shown in Fig. 1.

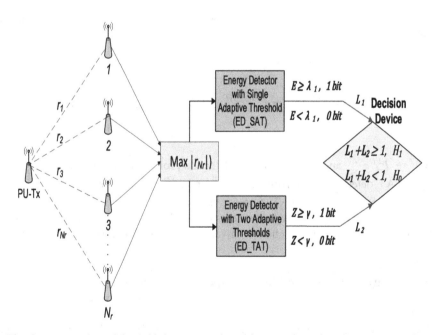

Fig. 1. Proposed Model: Multiple antennas based improved sensing detector (MA_ISD).

Suppose, $r_j(k)$ is the received PU signal at the jth antenna for the kth data stream, the total number of samples are N, the total number of antennas are N_r, and the channel between PU and CR is Rayleigh fading channel. Therefore, the output of the SC can be written as

$$SC|_{o/p} = max \sum_{j=1}^{N_r} \left[\sum_{k=1}^{N} |r_j(k)|^2 \right] \tag{3}$$

Figure 1 illustrates that the cognitive radio implies multiple antennas, out of multiple branches CR selects the antenna's branch that has a large gain and passes to detectors for further process.

- Probability of detection of multiple antennas based improved sensing detector can be defined as

$$P_D^{MA\_ISD} = P_r \times P_d^{ED\_SAT} + (1 - P_r) \times P_d^{ED\_TAT} + \frac{P_r}{2} \tag{4}$$

$$P_D^{MA\_ISD} = P_r \left(\frac{1}{2} + P_d^{ED\_SAT} - P_d^{ED\_TAT} \right) + P_d^{ED\_TAT} \tag{5}$$

- Total Error Probability of multiple antennas based improved sensing detector can be defined as

$$P_e^{MA\_ISD} = P_F^{MA\_ISD} + \left(1 - P_D^{MA\_ISD} \right) \tag{6}$$

$$P_e^{MA\_ISD} = P_r \left(P_f^{ED\_SAT} - P_f^{ED\_TAT} - P_d^{ED\_SAT} + P_d^{ED\_TAT} \right) + P_f^{ED\_TAT} \\ - P_d^{ED_{TAT}} + 1 \tag{7}$$

Where, $P_d^{ED\_SAT}$ and $P_d^{ED\_TAT}$ are the detection probability throughout of ED_SAT and ED_TAT detector respectively, $P_f^{ED\_SAT}$ and $P_f^{ED\_TAT}$ are the false alarm probability of ED_SAT and ED_TAT detector respectively. P_r is the probability factor, ranges $0 \leq P_r \leq 1$. Probability factor depends on SNR of the channels to be detected if P_r is less than 0.5 means the channel is very noisy, and vice-versa shows channel is less noisy.

3.1.1 Energy Detector with Single Adaptive Threshold (ED_SAT)

Energy detector is one of the most popular and usually used detectors by researchers to detect PU signals.

Figure 2 shows the picture of conventional-ED in which band pass filter (BPF) receives incoming PU signal and passes to analog to digital converter (ADC) after filtration. ADC converts an analog signal to digital signal and provides binary bit patterns. These binary bit patterns fed to square law device (SLD), who computes the energy of the received input signals. Further, integrator receives the

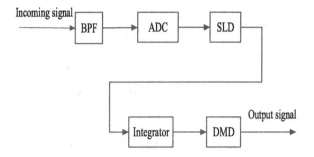

Fig. 2. Energy detector with single adaptive threshold (ED_SAT).

output of SLD and integrates at T interval. Finally, decision-making device (DMD) takes the final decision against incoming input signal with the help of single threshold value to confirm whether PU is present or absent.

3.1.1.1 Expression of Single Adaptive Threshold

The mathematical expression of single adaptive threshold (λ_1) can be defined as [11]

$$\lambda_1 = \left[N \times N_r \times \sigma_\omega^2 \left\{ Q^{-1} \left(\overline{P_f} \right) \times \sqrt{\frac{2}{N \times N_r}} + 1 \right\} \right] \tag{8}$$

Where, N is a number of samples, $Q^{-1}()$ denotes inverse- Q-function, P_f is false alarm probability, and σ_ω^2 is noise variance. Analyze Eq. (8), the threshold (λ_1) is directly proportional to noise variance (σ_ω^2), noise variance depends on noise signal, and the noise signal is random in nature and change w.r.t. time, due to this noise variance (σ_ω^2) varies, and then threshold (λ_1) also change. The threshold is adaptive in nature, therefore, at every time instant its value changes.

$$E = \frac{1}{N} \sum_{n=1}^{N} |r(n)|^2 \tag{9}$$

In the above Eq. (9), $r(n)$ is received signals, N is total numbers of samples and E represents the observed energy of $r(n)$. Finally, the local decision of ED_SAT detector can be defined as

$$\text{ED\_SAT}|_{\text{o/p}} = \begin{cases} E < \lambda_1, & bit\,0 = L_1 \\ E \geq \lambda_1, & bit\,1 = L_1 \end{cases} \tag{10}$$

3.1.1.2.1 Probability of Detection for ED_SAT Detector
The final expression for detection probability can be written as [5]

$$P_d^{ED\_SAT} = Q\left[\sqrt{\frac{N \times N_r}{2}} \times \left(\frac{\lambda'}{N \times N_r} - 1\right)\right] \tag{11}$$

In Eq. (11), N is numbers of samples, $Q()$ denotes Gaussian tail probability Q-function, and λ' is defined as $\lambda' = \frac{\lambda_1}{(\sigma_x^2 + \sigma_\omega^2)}$, where, λ_1 is a single adaptive threshold, σ_x^2 is PU signal variance, and σ_ω^2 is noise variance.

3.1.1.2.2 Probability of False Alarm for ED_SAT Detector

The final mathematical expression of false alarm probability can be derived as [5]

$$P_f^{ED\_SAT} = Q\left[\sqrt{\frac{N \times N_r}{2}} \times \left(\frac{\lambda''}{N \times N_r} - 1\right)\right] \tag{12}$$

In Eq. (12), N is a number of samples, and λ'' is defined as

$$\lambda'' = \frac{\lambda_1}{(\sigma_\omega^2)}.$$

3.1.1.2.3 Total Error Probability for ED_SAT Detector

The total error rate is the sum of the false alarm (P_f) and the missed-detection probability (P_m). Hence, the total error probability rate as follows [12]

$$P_e^{ED\_SAT} = \left(P_m^{ED\_SAT}\right) + P_f^{ED\_SAT} \tag{13}$$

Where, $(1-P_d)$ shows the missed-detection probability (P_m), then

$$P_e^{ED\_SAT} = Q\left[\sqrt{\frac{N \times N_r}{2}} \times \left(\frac{\lambda''}{N \times N_r} - 1\right)\right] \\ + \left(1 - Q\left[\sqrt{\frac{N \times N_r}{2}} \times \left(\frac{\lambda'}{N \times N_r} - 1\right)\right]\right) \tag{14}$$

3.1.2 Energy Detector with Two Adaptive Thresholds (ED_TAT)

In CRN, this is very difficult situation for a detector to detect correct signal while noise and PU signal overlap to each other this phenomenon is called sensing failure problem and overlapped area is called confused region, as discussed in [6]. To overcome this problem proposed MA_ISD sensing scheme is one of the fruitful solutions.

Generally, in CRN, there are three sections, in first section only noise signal exist denoted by H_0, in second only PU signal exist denoted by H_1, and third is the combination of noise and PU signal i.e. *confused region*. Figure 3(a) shows the case for C-ED where authors assume confused region is zero or null and simply divide all the sections into two parts using single threshold (γ) concept, H_1 if observed energy is greater than or equal to γ, and H_0 if observed energy is smaller than γ. Whereas, in Fig. 3(b) we have considered confused region and divided all the sections into four parts, below the γ_1 and above the γ_2 comes under upper part (UP) of the detector, while between $\gamma_1 - \gamma$ and $\gamma - \gamma_2$ is lower part (LP). Therefore, the detector output can be written as

$$ED\_TAT \big|_{o/p} = UP + LP = Z \tag{15}$$

Suppose, the observed energy is less than pre-defined threshold γ_1 it shows H_0, and H_1 if observed energy is greater than or equal to pre-defined threshold γ_2. But, for the confused region, if observed energy exists between $(\gamma_1 - \gamma)$ it shows 01 and further converts binary di-bits into decimal i.e. 1, similarly, if observed energy exists between $(\gamma - \gamma_2)$, shows 10 and further its decimal value is 2. Now, the pre-defined threshold (γ) can be calculated as [12]

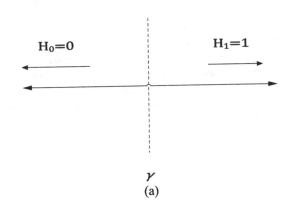

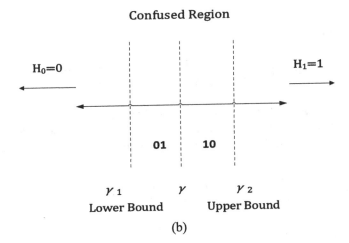

Fig. 3. (a) Single threshold detection scheme, and (b) double threshold detection scheme.

$$\gamma = \left[\left(\frac{N}{\sigma_\omega^2} \right) \times \left\{ Q^{-1} \left(\frac{-}{P_f} \right) \times \sqrt{\frac{2}{N}} + 1 \right\} \right] \tag{16}$$

The value of lower threshold (γ_1) and the upper threshold (γ_2) depends on noise variance, therefore, minimum noise variance shows lower threshold and maximum noise variance shows upper threshold. Now, the lower thresholds (γ_1) and upper threshold (γ_2) can be found as

$$\gamma_1 = \left[\left(\frac{N}{\rho \times \sigma_\omega^2} \right) \times \left\{ Q^{-1} (\overline{P_f}) \times \sqrt{\frac{2}{N}} + 1 \right\} \right] \tag{17}$$

$$\gamma_2 = \left[(N \times \rho \times \sigma_\omega^2) \times \left\{ Q^{-1} (\overline{P_f}) \times \sqrt{\frac{2}{N}} + 1 \right\} \right] \tag{18}$$

Equations (17) and (18) represent the mathematical expression of lower threshold (γ_1) and upper thresholds (γ_2) respectively. Now, considering the above equations i.e. (17) and (18), in both equations the thresholds (γ_1 & γ_2) depend on noise variance (σ_ω^2), and noise variance is variable because its value changes according to the noise signal. Due to this, the values of thresholds also change. Therefore, the thresholds are known as adaptive thresholds. The newly built sub-regions are ($\gamma_1\gamma - \gamma\gamma_2$) which comes under LP can be chosen as

$$LP = \begin{cases} if\ \gamma_1 \leq E < \gamma, & represent\ bit\ 01 \\ if\ \gamma \leq E < \gamma_2, & represent\ bit\ 10 \end{cases} \tag{19}$$

$$UP = \begin{cases} if\ E < \gamma_1, & represent\ bit\ 0 \\ if\ \gamma_2 \leq E, & represent\ bit\ 1 \end{cases} \tag{20}$$

Hence, the combination of LP and UP represents the local decision of ED_TAT detector [13, 14]

$$ED\_TAT|_{o/p} = \begin{cases} (UP + LP) < \gamma, & bit\ 0 = L_2 \\ (UP + LP) \geq \gamma, & bit\ 1 = L_2 \end{cases} \tag{21}$$

3.1.2.1.1 Probability of Detection for ED_TAT Detector
Assuming that $r(n)$ is a received sample whose normalized version is denoted by r_i. Now, the cumulative distribution function (CDF) of the ED_TAT, can be calculated as

$$f_{Zi}(z) = Pr\left(|r_i| \leq \sqrt{\left(z^{\frac{2}{a}} \right)} \right) \tag{22}$$

In Eq. (22), $P_r(\cdot)$ represents the probability. a is an arbitrary constant, has value two. By using the conditional probability density function (P.D.F.) of $|r_i|^2$ in Eq. (22) and after some algebra, we get the conditional P.D.F. of Z_i under hypothesis H_1, as [13]

$$f_{Z_i|H_j}(z) = \left[\frac{2 \times z^{\left(\frac{2}{a}\right)}}{(z \times a)}\right] \times f_{|r_i|^2|H_j}\left(z^{\left(\frac{2}{a}\right)}\right) \tag{23}$$

Where, $f_{|r_i|^2|H_1}$ is exponentially distributed as follows [13]

$$f_{|r_i|^2|H_1}(z) = \left[(1+S)^{-1}\right] \times exp\left[-z \times (1+S)^{-1}\right], z \geq 0 \tag{24}$$

Note that $S = (\sigma_h^2 \times \sigma_x^2)/\sigma_w^2$ represents the average SNR of the sensing channel. Finally, by using Eqs. (23) and (24) we have

$$f_{Z_i|H_1}(z) = \left[\frac{2 \times z^{\left(\frac{2}{a}\right)} \times (1+S)^{-1}}{(z \times a)}\right] \times exp\left[-z^{\left(\frac{2}{a}\right)} \times (1+S)^{-1}\right], z \geq 0 \tag{25}$$

Now, the detection probability for ED-TAT can be obtained as

$$P_d^{ED\_TAT} = \int_{\gamma}^{+\infty} f_{Z_i|H_1}(z)dz \tag{26}$$

$$P_d^{ED\_TAT} = \int_{\gamma}^{+\infty} \left[\frac{2 \times z^{\left(\frac{2}{a}\right)}}{(z \times a) \times (1+S)}\right] \times exp\left[-\frac{z^{\left(\frac{2}{a}\right)}}{(1+S)}\right]dz \tag{27}$$

$$P_d^{ED\_TAT} = exp\left[-\frac{\left\{(\gamma)^{\frac{1}{a}}\right\}^2}{(1+S)}\right] \tag{28}$$

3.1.2.1.2 Probability of False Alarm for ED_TAT Detector

Considering Eq. (23), $f_{|r_i|^2|H_0}$ is exponentially distributed as follows

$$f_{|r_i|^2|H_0}(z) = exp[-z], \quad z \geq 0 \tag{29}$$

Finally, by using Eqs. (23) and (29) we have

$$f_{Z_i|H_0}(z) = \left[\frac{2 \times z^{\left(\frac{2}{a}\right)}}{(z \times a)}\right] \times exp\left(z^{\left(\frac{2}{a}\right)}\right), \quad z \geq 0 \tag{30}$$

The false alarm probability for ED_TAT will be calculated as

$$P_f^{ED\_TAT} = \int\limits_{\gamma}^{+\infty} f_{Zi|H_o}(z)dz \tag{31}$$

$$P_f^{ED\_TAT} = \int\limits_{\gamma}^{+\infty} \left[\frac{2 \times z^{\left(\frac{2}{a}\right)}}{(z \times a)} \right] \times exp\left(z^{\left(\frac{2}{a}\right)} \right) dz \tag{32}$$

$$P_f^{ED\_TAT} = exp\left[-\left\{ (\gamma)^{\frac{1}{a}} \right\}^2 \right] \tag{33}$$

3.1.2.1.3 Total Error Probability for ED_TAT Detector

According to IEEE 802.22, total error rate depends on false alarm (P_f) and missed-detection probability (P_m), defined as

$$P_e^{ED\_TAT} = P_f^{ED\_TAT} + \left(1 - P_d^{ED\_TAT} \right) \tag{34}$$

Substitution the value of $P_d^{ED\_TAT}$ from Eq. (28) and the value of $P_f^{ED\_TAT}$ from Eqs. (33) and (34) we get

$$P_e^{ED\_TAT} = 1 + exp\left[-\left\{ (\gamma)^{\frac{1}{a}} \right\}^2 \right] - exp\left[-\frac{\left\{ (\gamma)^{\frac{1}{a}} \right\}^2}{(1+S)} \right] \tag{35}$$

Where, $\left(1 - P_d^{ED\_TAT} \right)$ shows the missed-detection probability denoted by $\left(P_m^{ED\_TAT} \right)$.

3.1.3 Decision Device (DD)

This device takes final decision whether PU frequency band is free or not using OR-rule. DD depends on the output of ED_SAT (L_1) as shown in Eq. (10) and output of ED_TAT (L_2) as shown in Eq. (21). Now, the combination of L_1 and L_2 forms the final mathematical expression for the proposed model given as

$$DD = \begin{cases} L_1 \ OR \ L_2 \geq 1, & 1, \\ L_1 \ OR \ L_2 < 1, & 0, \end{cases} \tag{36}$$

Flow chart shows the flow of operation, Fig. 4, illustrates the working operation of MA_ISD technique. In the given figure, CR receiver senses the received signal and perform the respective sensing operations using ED_SAT and ED_TAT detectors, and further, makes a final decision via decision device (DD) that PU band is available or not.

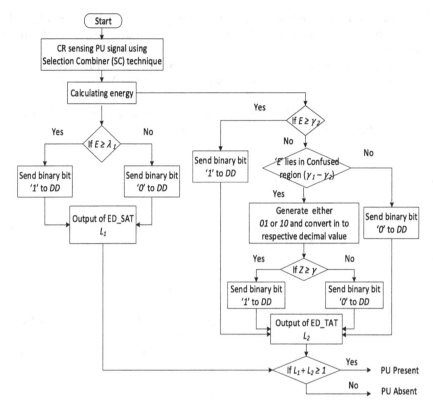

Fig. 4. Flow chart of MA_ISD technique.

- **Simulation model**

The simulation model is developed using MATLAB. Following are the simulation steps described as:

1. Generate QPSK modulated signal $x(n)$.
2. Pass input $x(n)$ signal through a noisy channel, channel is Rayleigh, having channel gain (h), and noise is AWGN (additive white gaussian noise) denoted by $\omega(n)$ having zero mean i.e. $\omega(n) \sim N (0, \sigma^2_\omega)$, & σ^2_ω is noise variance, according to Eq. (1).
3. CR users contain a selection combiner (SC) that provides maximum SNR value signal out of N_r decision statistics, according to Eq. (3).
4. The received signal $r(n)$ receive by CR users are defined as $\omega(n)$ under the null hypothesis, and $x(n)*h(n) + \omega(n)$ under alternate hypothesis.
5. Calculate thresholds λ_1, γ, γ_1, and γ_2 according to Eqs. (8, 16, 17 and 18) for fixed probability of false alarm $P_f = 0.1$.
6. Calculate test statistics (E) according to Eq. (9).

7. Compare E with thresholds λ_1, γ_1, γ_2, and γ of step 5, to claim hypothesis H_0 (0 bit) or H_1 (1 bit) or generate one-bit decision L_1 or L_2 according to Eqs. (10) and (21) respectively.
8. Add all statistics generate from step 7 according to Eq. (36) and compare with threshold 1 by using hard decision *OR-Rule* for fixed probability of false alarm $P_f = 0.1$.
9. Steps 1–8 are repeated 1000 times to evaluate the detection probability vs SNR under constraints that false alarm probability is set at 0.1.

3.2 Multiple Antennas Based Centralized Spectrum Sensing (MA_CSS) Technique

CSS technique is useful to enhance detection performance of CR users because it reduces fading and shadowing effect problems [15]. In CSS, centralized-cooperative SS technique is better than de-centralized because it is more reliable and accurate [7]. In the centralized-CSS technique, there is a single fusion center (FC) who collects the local decision (in the form of single-binary bits either 0 or 1) of CR users and forms a final decision using decision rules.

In Fig. 5, let there are k numbers of CR users and local binary (bit 0 or 1) decision O_i of all CR users have been collected by a common single center known as FC. FC collects data and performs *OR-rule* hard decision to decide the presence or absence of PU spectrum band.

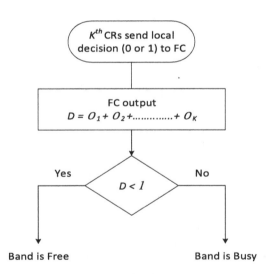

Fig. 5. Flow chart of MA_CSS technique.

$$D = \sum_{i=1}^{k} O_i \tag{37}$$

Now, O_i can be expressed in terms of pre-defined threshold (γ), hence the final expression will be

$$O_i = \begin{cases} 1, & L_1 + L_1 \geq 1 \\ 0, & L_1 + L_1 < 1 \end{cases} \tag{38}$$

In Eq. (37), D is the sum of all local binary decisions O_i sent by i^{th} CR users. O_i is the output of proposed MA_ISD model shown in Eq. (36). If thresholds (γ) is greater than calculated energy levels, it indicates the channel is free otherwise busy. In functional representation form the FC expression for global decision can be written as

$$FD = \begin{cases} 0, & \sum_{i=1}^{k} O_i < 1 \\ 1, & \sum_{i=1}^{k} O_i \geq 1 \end{cases} \tag{39}$$

$$FD = \begin{cases} D < 1, & H_0 \\ D \geq 1, & H_1 \end{cases} \tag{40}$$

Equation (40) shows the final decision of FC in terms of D using Eq. (39). Therefore, the detection probability of centralized-CSS using hard decision *OR-rule* can be expressed as follows

$$P_D = P_r \left\{ \sum_{j=1}^{k} O_i \geq 1 | H_1 \right\} \tag{41}$$

$$P_D = 1 - \prod_{j=1}^{k} \left(1 - P_{d,j} \right) \tag{42}$$

In Eq. (42), P_d is the detection probability of individual CR users that is computed using Eq. (5). Further, the proposed cooperative sensing scheme can be explained with the help of flow chart given in Fig. 5.

- **Simulation model**

The simulation model is developed using MATLAB. Following are the simulation steps described as:

10. Steps 1–9 are repeated, local decision generated by CRs according to Eq. (38) and sent to FC.
11. FC collects CR users output according to Eq. (37).

12. Apply hard decision *OR-rule* at FC output according to Eq. (40), to claim hypothesis H_0 or H_1.
13. Steps 10–12 are repeated 1000 times to evaluate the detection probability vs SNR under constraints that false alarm probability is set at 0.1.

4   Numerical Results and Analysis

In our simulations, we first evaluate the systems using QPSK modulation scheme and Rayleigh channel. In this section, the proposed MA_ISD scheme is compared with conventional energy detection, ED and cyclostationary-2010 detection [3], Adaptive spectrum sensing-2012 [4], and energy detection technique for adaptive spectrum sensing-2015 (EDT-ASS-2015) [5]. The parameters used for simulation are given in Table 1.

Table 1. Parameter values for simulation.

Parameter	Value
Signal type	QPSK
Channel (between primary users and cognitive radio users)	Rayleigh
Number of samples (N)	1000
Number of Antennas (N_r)	3 & 2
Threshold (λ_1)	1.25
Threshold (γ)	1.014
Threshold (γ_1)	0.9
Threshold (γ_2)	1.2
Range of signal to noise ratio	−20 dB to 0 dB
Probability of false alarm for each detection scheme	0.1
Software	MATLAB R2012a

In the following simulation given in Fig. 6, we employ the MA_ISD technique for 1000 numbers of samples, we set the threshold for the system to achieve false alarm probability 0.1. In the simulation environment, the value of λ_1, γ, γ_1, and γ_2 varies at every iteration. But in this case we have chosen $\lambda_1 = 1.25$, $\gamma_1 = 0.9$, $\gamma_2 = 1.2$ and $\gamma = 1.014$ as trade-off value.

In simulation environment, there is detection performance comparison between proposed a multiple antennas based improved sensing detector (MA_ISD) scheme, EDT-ASS-2015 scheme, ED and cyclo-2010, adaptive SS-2012, and conventional-ED scheme. Analysis Fig. 6, proposed MA_ISD scheme with number of antennas (N_r) = 3 outperforms $N_r = 1$, 2, EDT-ASS-2015 scheme, ED and cyclo-2010, adaptive SS-2012, and conventional-ED scheme by 9.0%, 4.5%, 29.1%, 57.9%, 42.4%, & 54.1% at −12 dB SNR in terms of detection probability respectively.

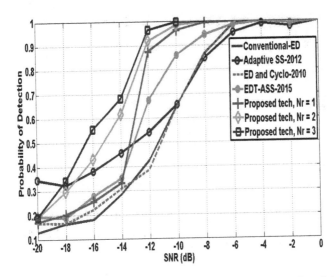

Fig. 6. Detection probability with respect to SNR values at $P_f = 0.1$.

According to IEEE 802.22, if false alarm probability is set at 0.1 then the acceptance value of detection probability must be 0.9. It shows that MA_ISD scheme detects PU signal at approximately −12.5 dB SNR.

Figure 7 shows the performance of proposed MA_ISD scheme using same parameters in terms of Total Error Probability. Figure 7 shows that the proposed technique with $N_r = 3$ has minimum error rate i.e. 0.1 at −10 dB SNR while for the same error probability other techniques have large SNR rate.

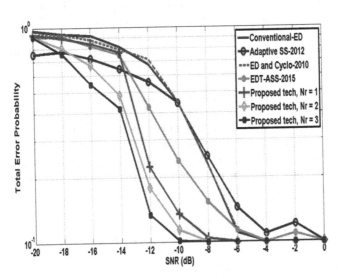

Fig. 7. Probability of error with respect to SNR values.

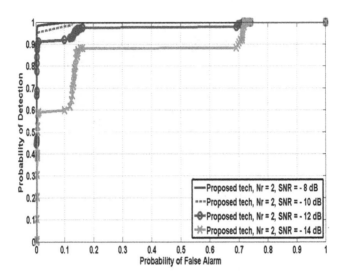

Fig. 8. ROC Curves for MA_ISD spectrum sensing detector under different SNR values.

Receiver Operating Characteristics (ROC) curve shows the behavior of P_d with respect to P_f [16]. According to IEEE 802.22, the value of detection probability should be large at minimum P_f value. In the next step of the simulations given in Fig. 8, we perform a system employing QPSK modulation scheme. First, we investigate how detection probability changes with respect to false alarm probability.

Thus, we evaluate our simulations for different false alarm probabilities while SNR is −8, −10, −12 & −14 dB and 1000 samples are applied to proposed MA_ISD scheme. In this figure, it is straightforwardly seen that less false alarm probability leads more detection probability. Then, we decide to keep our following simulations for $P_f = 0.1$, $N_r = 2$, and SNR −12 dB, detection probability is close to 0.9 i.e. 0.9110, this is acceptable for licensed signal detection as per IEEE 802.22 norms [17].

The spectrum sensing or detection time is the time taken by CR users to detect licensed frequency band. Sensing time can be computed as

$$T_{MA\_ISD} = T_{SC} + min.\,(T_{ED\_SAT}, T_{ED\_TAT} + T_{DD}) \tag{43}$$

In Eq. (43), T_{MA_ISD} is total time taken by proposed sensing technique for SS. T_{SC}, T_{ED_SAT} and T_{ED_TAT} are the selection combiner (SC), ED_SAT and ED_TAT detectors SS time respectively. In Fig. 1, ED_SAT and ED_TAT are placed parallel, therefore, we take minimum time out of the two detectors as shown in Eq. (43). Now, the sensing time for SC can be calculated as

$$T_{SC} = C \times \frac{1}{2} \times \left(\frac{M_{SC}}{B}\right) \tag{44}$$

In Eq. (44), M_{SC} is the samples, B is the bandwidth of the channel for SC, and number of sensed channels denoted by C. Now, the ED_SAT sensing time can be calculated as

$$T_{ED\_SAT} = C \times P_r \times \frac{1}{2} \times \left(\frac{M_{ED\_SAT}}{B}\right) \tag{45}$$

In Eq. (45), M_{ED_SAT} is the samples and P_r is probability factor for the ED_SAT detector. Similarly, the ED_TAT detector sensing time can be calculated as

$$T_{ED\_TAT} = C \times (1 - Pr) \times \frac{1}{2} \times \left(\frac{M_{ED\_TAT}}{B}\right) \tag{46}$$

In Eq. (46), M_{ED_TAT} is the samples and $(1 - P_r)$ is the probability factor for the ED_TAT detector. The decision device (DD) sensing time can be calculated as

$$T_{DD} = C \times \frac{1}{2} \times \left(\frac{M_0}{B}\right) \tag{47}$$

In Eq. (47), M_0 is the samples of DD. Therefore, the overall spectrum sensing time can be computed using Eqs. (43), (44), (45), (46) and (47) as

$$
\begin{aligned}
T_{MA\_ISD} = &\frac{1}{2} \times \left(\frac{C}{B}\right) \times \{M_{SC} + M_0\} \\
&+ min. \left[\frac{1}{2} \times \left(\frac{C}{B}\right) \times \{P_r \times M_{ED\_SAT}, \quad (1 - P_r) \times M_{ED\_TAT}\}\right]
\end{aligned}
\tag{48}
$$

Figure 9 shows the graph between sensing time and SNR. IEEE 802.22 suggested that the time taken by CR users during the detection of PU spectrum bands for spectrum sensing should be as small as possible. Analyze Fig. 9, it can be concluded that the presented detection scheme at $N_r = 2$ yields minimum detection time as compared to existing schemes. Meanwhile, the value of detection time decreases as SNR increases, therefore there is an inverse relationship between both of them. We have used Eq. (48) for plotting the graph between sensing time and SNR. The value of parameters used in Eq. (48) is defined in Table 1.

SNR = −20 dB SNR, proposed scheme at $N_r = 2$ takes approximately 46.7 ms time to detect PU signal while presently existing schemes (EDT-ASS-2015, Adaptive SS-2012, ED and Cyclo-2010) require around 47.0 ms, 49.0 ms, and 53.2 ms sensing time respectively. Given graph shows that proposed scheme take time (i.e. 46.7 ms) at −20 dB which is better than other. The small detection time is available for transmissions while more time is dedicated to sensing, therefore, this degrades the CR throughput and this phenomenon is said to be the sensing efficiency problem [18, 19].

Figure 10 shows the curve between detection probability and Threshold value for four different SNR values such as −8 dB, −10 dB, −12 dB, & −14 dB.

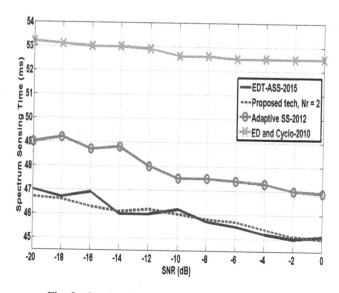

Fig. 9. Sensing Time with respect to SNR values.

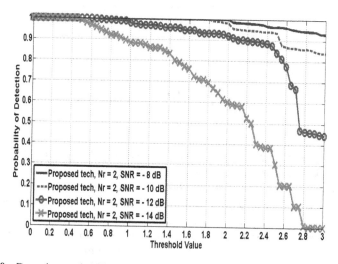

Fig. 10. Detection probability with respect to threshold values for different SNRs.

It concludes that the presented MA_ISD SS scheme can detect licensed signal at −8 dB SNR at $N = 1000$, and $\lambda = 3.0$ with $N_r = 2$.

Figure 11 shows the graph of detection probability (P_d) versus SNR between proposed CSS with MA_ISD scheme, CSS-EDT-ASS-2015, and Hierarchical with Quantization-2012 scheme. In CSS, assumed there are three numbers of CR users and two numbers of antennas. Simulation results indicate that CSS with MA_ISD outperforms EDT-ASS-2015, and Hierarchical with quantization-2012 by 12.5% & 19.1%

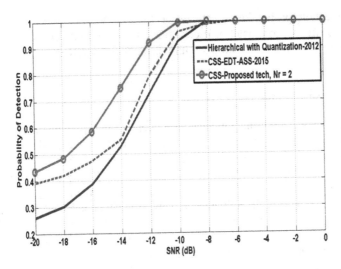

Fig. 11. Detection probability with respect to SNR values at $N_r = 2$ and total CR users $k = 3$.

at −12 dB SNR respectively. CSS with MA_ISD achieves 0.9 detection probability at −12.5 dB with $N_r = 2$, while EDT-ASS-2015 and Hierarchical with quantization-2012 detection scheme achieves the same detection probability at −11 dB & −10.5 dB respectively.

In Fig. 12, as the numbers of CR users increase detection probability improve. In the given simulation environment, we set P_f at 0.1, and take the number of cooperative CR users $k = 3, 4, 5, 6, 7, 8, 9$ & 10, $N_r = 2$, and $N = 1000$. It shows that the optimize

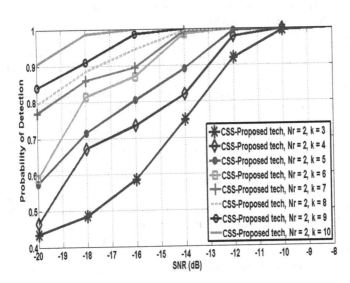

Fig. 12. Probability of Detection Vs SNR at $P_f = 0.1$ with $N = 1000$, total CR users $k = 3, 4, 5, 6, 7, 8, 9, 10$, QPSK modulation scheme and Rayleigh fading channel.

value of detection probability outcomes at $k = 10$, $N_r = 2$, under $P_f = 0.1$, when SNR = −20.0 dB (approximately). It concludes that proposed detector can detect PU spectrum band at or below −20.0 dB with ten numbers of CR users.

5 Conclusion

In this paper, a novel multiple antennas based centralized spectrum sensing technique has been proposed. This scheme enhances detection performance, reduces bit error rate as well as detection time. Numerical results confirm that proposed MA_ISD scheme while $N_r = 2$ outperforms other existing schemes (i.e. EDT-ASS-2015 scheme, ED and cyclo-2010, adaptive SS-2012, and conventional-ED scheme), by 24.6%, 53.4%, 37.9%, and 49.6% at −12 dB SNR respectively. It is also confirmed that the presented scheme yields lesser detection time than EDT-ASS-2015, Adaptive SS-2012, and ED and Cyclo-2010 scheme in the order of 47.0 ms, 49.0 ms, and 53.2 ms at −20 dB SNR respectively. MA_ISD has also been implemented with CSS scheme, it further confirms that $k = 10$, $N_r = 2$, and $P_f = 0.1$, presented sensing scheme detects licensed signal as per IEEE 802.22 at very low SNR i.e. −20 dB SNR.

Acknowledgment. The authors wish to thank their parents for supporting and motivating for this work because without their blessings and God's grace this was not possible.

References

1. Federal Communications Commission, Notice of proposed rule making and order: Facilitating opportunities for flexible, efficient, and reliable spectrum use employing cognitive radio technologies, ET Docket No. 03-108, February 2005
2. Bagwari, A., Singh, B.: Comparative performance evaluation of spectrum sensing techniques for cognitive radio networks. In: 2012 Fourth IEEE International Conference on Computational Intelligence and Communication Networks (CICN- 2012), vol. 1, pp. 98–105 (2012)
3. Maleki, S., Pandharipande, A., Leus, G.: Two-Stage Spectrum sensing for cognitive radios. In: IEEE Conference on Acoustics Speech and Signal Processing (ICASSP), pp. 2946–2949 (2010)
4. Ejaz, W., Hasan, N., Kim, H.S.: SNR-based adaptive spectrum sensing for cognitive radio networks. Int. J. Innovative Comput. Inform. Control 8(9), 6095–6105 (2012)
5. Sobron, I., Diniz, P.S.R., Martins, W.A.: Velez, M: Energy detection technique for adaptive spectrum sensing. IEEE Trans. Commun. 63(3), 617–627 (2015)
6. Liu, S.-Q., Hu, B.-J., Wang, X.-Y.: Hierarchical cooperative spectrum sensing based on double thresholds energy detection. IEEE Commun. Lett. 16(7), 1096–1099 (2012)
7. Akyildiz, I.F., Lo, B.F., Balakrishnan, R.: Cooperative spectrum sensing in cognitive radio networks: a survey. Elsevier Phys. Commun. 4, 40–62 (2011)
8. Teguig, D., Scheers, B., Le Nir, V.: Data fusion schemes for cooperative spectrum sensing in cognitive radio networks. IEEE Trans. Wireless Commun. 7(4), 1326–1337 (2008)

9. Pandharipande, A., Linnartz, J.-P.M.G.: Performance analysis of primary user detection in a multiple antenna cognitive radio. In: Proceedings of the IEEE International Conference on Communications, pp. 6482–6486 (2007)
10. Taherpour, A., Nasiri-Kenari, M., Gazor, S.: Multiple antenna spectrum sensing in cognitive radios. IEEE Trans. Wireless Commun. 9(2), 814–823 (2010)
11. Tandra, R., Sahai, A.: SNR walls for signal detection. IEEE J. Sel. Topic Sig. Proc. 2(1), 4–16 (2008)
12. Bagwari, A., Kanti, J., Singh, G., Tomar, A.S.: Reliable spectrum sensing scheme based on dual detector with double-threshold for IEEE 802.22 WRAN. J. High Speed Netw. 21(3), 205–220 (2015). IOS Press
13. Singh, A., Bhatnagar, M.R., Mallik, R.K.: Cooperative spectrum sensing in multiple antenna based cognitive radio network using an improved energy detector. IEEE Commun. Lett. 16 (1), 64–67 (2011)
14. Zhang, W., Letaief, K.B.: Cooperative spectrum sensing with transmit and relay diversity in cognitive radio networks. IEEE Trans. Wireless Commun. 7, 4761–4766 (2008)
15. Ganesan, G., Li, Y.(G.): Cooperative spectrum sensing in cognitive radio–part I: two user networks. IEEE Trans. Wireless Commun. 6(6), 2204–2213 (2007)
16. Zhang, L., Huang, J., Tang, C.: Novel energy detection scheme in cognitive radio. In: IEEE Conference on Signal Processing, Communications and Computing (ICSPCC), pp. 1–4 (2011)
17. Cordeiro, C., Challapali, K., Birru, D., Shankar, S.: IEEE 802.22: the first worldwide wireless standard based on cognitive radios. In: Proceedings of DySPAN 2005, November 2005
18. Lee, W.Y., Akyildiz, I.F.: Optimal spectrum sensing framework for cognitive radio networks. IEEE Trans. Wireless Commun. 7(10), 3845–3857 (2008)
19. Liang, Y.C., Zeng, Y., Peh, E., Hoang, A.T.: Sensing-throughput tradeoff for cognitive radio networks. IEEE Trans. Wireless Commun. 7(4), 1326–1337 (2008)

ImatiSTL - Fast and Reliable Mesh Processing with a Hybrid Kernel

Marco Attene[(⊠)]

IMATI CNR, Genova, Italy
marco.attene@ge.imati.cnr.it

Abstract. A novel approach is presented to deal with geometric computations while joining the efficiency of floating point representations with the robustness of exact arithmetic. Our approach is based on a hybrid geometric kernel where a floating point number is made fully interoperable with an exact rational number, so that the latter can be used only within critical parts of the program or within restricted portions of the input. The whole program can dynamically change the level of precision used to produce new values and to evaluate expressions. Around such a kernel, a mesh processing library has been implemented whose API functions can be classified depending on their precision as always exact, always approximated, or exact if the current level of precision is sufficient. Such a classification allows implementing algorithms with a full control of the robustness at an unprecedented level of granularity. Experiments show that this interoperability comes at a nearly negligible cost: on average, a test algorithm implemented on our hybrid kernel is just 8% slower than the same algorithm implemented on a *standard* floating point version of the same kernel while providing the possibility to be fully robust if necessary.

1 Introduction

Geometry processing involves a switch from the mathematical to the computational world where many developers simply approximate real numbers with floating point (FP) representations [1]. Most of the times this approach is accurate enough and efficient, and that is why numerous libraries and algorithms to perform geometric computations use FP numbers [2,3] to represent coordinates, distances, angles, etc. Unfortunately, FP operations are subject to roundoff error, and in some cases the result of a computation may become useless due to such a mismatch. Implementations that neglect this observation can be subject to failures, infinite loops, and crashes.

1.1 Exact and Multi-precision Arithmetic

To ensure that all the computations lead to exact results one may rely on exact or multi-precision arithmetic libraries [4–6]. This solution is extremely robust, and in most cases the available memory is the only limitation. Unfortunately, working

© Springer-Verlag GmbH Germany 2017
M.L. Gavrilova and C.J. Kenneth Tan (Eds.): Trans. on Comput. Sci. XXIX, LNCS 10220, pp. 86–96, 2017.
DOI: 10.1007/978-3-662-54563-8_5

with exact representations has a significant impact on the performances, and a program might become even twenty times slower than its corresponding FP-based version [7]. This makes this solution unpractical in many cases, especially when large datasets must be elaborated with guarantees.

1.2   Arithmetic Filtering

The correctness of some algorithms is solely based on the exact evaluation of a specific predicate that can assume one of a small set of values (e.g. true/false, $1/0/-1$, ...). If the arithmetic expression that leads to the predicate's value is subject to roundoff, one can rely on the so-called "filtered arithmetic" approach. Roughly speaking, the roundoff's potential magnitude is assessed, and only if it is sufficient to make the final result switch from one value to another (e.g. from true to false or vice versa), then the predicate is evaluated using a more accurate though slower approach. In several practical cases, FP numbers are accurate enough for the vast majority of the predicate evaluations, thus this approach combines the efficiency of FP computations with the robustness of exact arithmetic. A noticeable example of this technique is due to Shewchuk [2], who introduced fast and robust predicates to evaluate the incircle test needed to compute Delaunay triangulations. As a rule of thumb, the filtered arithmetic approach is appropriate when all the predicate expressions are direct functions of input values.

1.3   Lazy Evaluation

For some algorithms, however, a predicate might be necessarily a function of some intermediate values. If these values incorporate a roundoff error, the predicates's evaluation cannot be guaranteed to be correct even when using filtered arithmetic. To cope with these cases one can still revert to exact arithmetic and compute intermediate values without error but, once again, this easily leads to unacceptably slow implementations. Alternatively, instead of representing intermediate values explicitly, one may encode the symbolic expressions to be used for their evaluation. In other words, an intermediate value can be encoded within a Direct Acyclic Graph (DAG) representing a specific function of input values. When a predicate must be evaluated, such an expression is combined with the expression of the predicate itself, and filtered arithmetic can be used to exactly derive the result. Due to this inherent procrastination, this approach is usually called "lazy evaluation". Lazy evaluation is particularly useful to compute mesh booleans, where new points representing the intersection of edges and triangles are used to derive the result [8]. This approach is typically combined with filtered arithmetic: a DAG representing the number's exact history is coupled with an interval containing its exact value and an FP number within that interval. When a number is used in a predicate expression, its interval is exploited to perform the filtering: if the test passes, the predicate is evaluated using FP arithmetic, otherwise the evaluation is done based on the DAGs. The main drawback of this approach is due to the need of the DAGS: these structures, indeed, have a relatively large memory footprint and their update and management have an inevitable impact on the performances.

1.4 Mixed Techniques

One of the most diffused forms of exact arithmetic uses rational numbers with arbitrarily large numerator and denominator [5]. Since this solution is only suitable to model problems where no irrational numbers are involved, in some existing libraries [6,7] values derived from irrational operations (e.g. square root) are stored in symbolic form as done in the lazy evaluation approach. Clearly, the evaluation of expressions that involve such "irrational" numbers might become slower. In the scope of this paper, however, we shall not deal with irrational expressions.

1.5 CGAL

The Computational Geometry Algorithm Library (CGAL) is one of the few existing tools which includes all the aforementioned techniques to deal with robustness, and can be considered as a representative of the state of the art in robust geometric computing. In particular, CGAL provides a special templated number type called Lazy_exact_nt<NT> to implement the aforementioned lazy evaluation on a basic number type NT [9]. In essence, approximated values are used instead of NT as long as possible, but the computational history is maintained within the DAG and evaluated if needed. Hence, when NT is a slow exact type this approach can significantly speed up the computation.

For more comprehensive overviews of geometric robustness and related issues, see Yap [10] and Goldberg [11].

1.6 Key Contribution

Existing libraries allow developers to choose among various number types and computational kernels. For example, if the program needs guarantees about the relative position of projected points, exact coordinates must be used; if the program must just visualize a mesh, FP numbers are sufficient. But what if the program needs to do both? Typically, the number type is chosen once for the entire program based on the maximum precision required. If such a maximum precision is required only by a small percentage of the operations, most of the program is unnecessarily slowed down and memory-intensive, even if lazily-evaluated types are used.

Conversely, in ImatiSTL the developer may freely switch from one kernel to another while being guaranteed that all the numbers remain compatible and interoperable with each other, with significant advantages in terms of both speed and memory consumption as shown in Sect. 4. This result could be achieved thanks to the definition and implementation of a novel *hybrid* number type, whose advantages with respect to the state of the art (i.e. CGAL) are described in the following Sect. 2.

2   Hybrid Number Type

CGAL's lazy evaluation and filtered arithmetic must determine an interval containing the exact result of an expression [9]. However, computing such an interval has its own cost, and this makes the approach really beneficial only when (1) there is an actual need of exact evaluations and (2) such a need is rare with respect to the total amount of the expressions to be evaluated. Based on these observations, a developer must determine whether his/her algorithm is worth to be implemented on a lazily-evaluated number type and, if so, the program must be configured accordingly. To do this, existing libraries such as CGAL require specifying a number type and a computational kernel, and dynamically changing these settings while the program executes is quite unpractical (i.e. all the numbers involved should be explicitly converted to the new type, which has an impact on both development effort and program efficiency). Therefore, though a developer might know exactly where the program requires exactness, both in terms of computational flow and in terms of input data, such an information can be hardly exploited. To overcome this limitation, in the remainder we define a novel polymorphic number type that has virtually the same performances of a standard double precision floating point, but can encode either an actual floating point or an exact number. Differently from CGAL's Lazy_exact_nt, the user can explicitly control the need of exactness when operating with our polymorphic numbers: this makes it possible to avoid unnecessary interval computations and checks to speed up the program when approximated results are known to be enough.

2.1   Terminology and Definition

In the remainder, a standard IEEE double precision floating point number is shortly called an "FP number". An FP number has an encoding and a value: the former is just a fixed-sized sequence of bits, while the latter is an element of the set of rational numbers Q. According to IEEE 754 standard specifications, any encoding corresponds to a unique value, though the vice-versa is not necessarily true (e.g. the encoding for the value 0.25 changes if the number is represented as $25 * 10^{-2}$ or as $250 * 10^{-3}$). FP numbers can encode a finite subset of the rational numbers. However, since rational numbers form an enumerable set, it is reasonable to look for a more comprehensive encoding. This observation led to the development of libraries such as GMP and LEDA, where any rational value is encoded as a pair of arbitrarily large integers representing the numerator and denominator.

Herewith a new number type called *PM_Rational* is introduced whose encoding is inherently polymorphic. Any rational number can be represented as a PM_Rational (up to memory limits), but its encoding might be either an FP number or a pair numerator/denominator. Independently of the actual encoding of the operands, arithmetic operations may be either exact or subject to roundoff, and the developer has the possibility to control this level of precision at any time. Essentially, the user acts on a global parameter that determines the precision level of the PM_Rational operations. Three levels are available: *approximated, filtered, precise*. When the *approximated* mode is active, all the expressions on PM_Rationals are computed just as if they were FP numbers with virtually no performance degradation with respect to native IEEE double precision arithmetic: in this mode predicates might assume a wrong value. In *filtered* mode, PM_Rationals still behave as FP numbers, but predicates are evaluated using arithmetic filtering: in this mode predicates are guaranteed to assume the correct value, but expressions that produce other PM_Rationals might still lead to approximated evaluations: in other words, intermediate PM_Rational values are not guaranteed to be exact. Finally, in *precise* mode, all the predicates and rational expressions are guaranteed to be exactly evaluated.

Thanks to this paradigm, a program can load a geometric model such as a polygonal mesh and encode the vertex coordinates as PM_Rationals. This same mesh can be used for different processes with different precision levels without the need to perform explicit type conversions. For example, an *approximated* mode can be employed to render the mesh using backface culling. For this operation, indeed, it is reasonable to accept wrong orientations for triangles whose normal vector is nearly orthogonal to the line of sight. Then, the program can switch to *filtered* mode to perform *point_in_polyhedron* queries with a guaranteed correct result. A final switch to *precise* mode allows to exactly calculate and represent the intersection of the mesh with another model.

2.2   Implementation

Internally, the PM_Rational type has been implemented in C++ as a class containing one 64bit-sized generic *data* member, and one boolean *type* member that specifies what the *data* member encodes. In particular, the *data* member can encode either a standard IEEE double precision number (*type* = double) or a pointer to a pair numerator/denominator (*type* = rational). In its turn, a pair numerator/denominator is encoded as an *mpq_class* defined within the C++ interface to the GMP library. Note that the type of a PM_Rational number is independent of the global precision mode that the program employs at any time. The latter is encoded as a public static member called *Kernel_mode* that determines the current precision level to be used in the PM_Rational computations. *PM_Rational* :: *Kernel_mode* is essentially a global variable that the user can change at any time.

All the arithmetic and comparison operators are defined on PM_Rationals. For arithmetic operators (i.e. $+$, $-$, $*$, $/$, $+=$, $-=$, $*=$, $/=$), the current *Kernel_mode* is used to produce the result, independently of the type of the operands. Hence, the operation $A + B$ returns a PM_Rational whose type is double if the current *Kernel_mode* is either *approximated* or *filtered*, whereas the resulting type is rational if the mode is *precise*. If necessary, the operands are transparently converted to the type of the result before calling the corresponding native operator. Conversely, for comparison operators (i.e. $==$, $<$, $>$, $<=$, $>=$) the *type* of the operands is used to determine the result. If both the operands have the same *type* the native comparison operator for such a *type* is used. If they have different *type*, the operand having a double *type* is converted to rational and the native comparison for rationals is used.

3   ImatiSTL

A mesh processing library called ImatiSTL has been implemented to exploit the PM_Rational numbers. This library provides an API whose functions can be classified as follows:

- *Always exact* - the return value (or the processing result) is guaranteed to be reliable in any kernel mode. These functions include, e.g., coordinate comparison, vector inversion, operations on the connectivity graph.
- *Exact if kernel mode is filtered* - the return value (or the processing result) is guaranteed to be reliable only if kernel mode is at least set to *filtered*. Functions of this type normally involve orientation predicates (e.g. Delaunay triangulation of a 2D point set).
- *Exact if kernel mode is precise* - the return value (or the processing result) is guaranteed to be reliable only if kernel mode is set to *precise*. Functions of this type might involve intermediate values that influence the flow of the computation (e.g. relative position of projected points, intersections).
- *Always approximated* - the result of the function (or one of its intermediate values) does not necessarily belong to the set of rational numbers. Functions of this type normally involve Euclidean distances, angles, or other irrational quantities. Note that squared distances are implemented within the aforementioned class *Exact if kernel mode is precise*.

A set of geometric predicates has been implemented in ImatiSTL to exploit the inherent type polymorphism provided by PM_Rational coordinates. Any such predicate is a *friend* function of PM_Rational and proceeds to an appropriate computation depending both on the current *Kernel_mode* and on the *type* of the operands. Friendship is required because the predicates need to access the *type* member which is not part of the public interface. For example, the typical 2D orientation predicate is implemented as in Algorithm 1:
Note that all of this is transparent to the developer who is only required to change the kernel mode when necessary.

4   Results and Discussion

To test the actual behavior of the hybrid kernel, three different versions of the same algorithm have been implemented. The test algorithm creates a tetrahedron (Fig. 1(a)), performs five steps of Loop subdivision on it [12] (Fig. 1(b)), creates a copy of the so-subdivided tetrahedron and shifts it along the positive X axis (Fig. 1(c)), and calculates the outer hull of the resulting pair of intersecting models [8] (Fig. 1(d)). In the approximated version, the test algorithm uses an implementation of ImatiSTL where traditional double precision

---

Algorithm 1. Implementation of the planar orientation predicate. On lines 11–13 $Kernel\_mode$ is $filtered$ but at least one operand is $rational$.

Require: Three 2D points represented as pairs of PM_Rationals $P = (p_x, p_y)$, $Q = (q_x, q_y)$, $R = (r_x, r_y)$

Ensure: CCW, ALIGNED, CW, depending on the relative orientation of R wrt P and Q

1: PM_Rational O; // Temporary value to determine the predicate's output
2: **if** $Kernel\_mode$ is $approximated$ **then**
3:    $O = ((p_x - r_x) * (q_y - r_y) - (p_y - r_y) * (q_x - r_x))$
4: **else**
5:    **if** all the operands are of type $double$ **then**
6:       Compute O using filtered arithmetic as done in [2]
7:    **else**
8:       **if** $Kernel\_mode$ is $precise$ **then**
9:          $O = ((p_x - r_x) * (q_y - r_y) - (p_y - r_y) * (q_x - r_x))$
10:      **else**
11:         Temporarily switch to $precise$ $Kernel\_mode$
12:         $O = ((p_x - r_x) * (q_y - r_y) - (p_y - r_y) * (q_x - r_x))$
13:         Swicth back to $filtered$ $Kernel\_mode$
14:      **end if**
15:   **end if**
16: **end if**
17: **if** $O>0$ **then**
18:    return CCW
19: **else**
20:    **if** $O==0$ **then**
21:       return ALIGNED
22:    **else**
23:       return CW
24:    **end if**
25: **end if**

---

numbers are used to represent the coordinates. Similarly, in the exact version $CGAL :: Lazy\_exact\_nt < CGAL :: Gmpq >$ was used to represent the coordinates. In the hybrid version, PM_Rational was used instead. The following three indicators were measured: number of source code lines used to implement the test program (ImatiSTL library not included in the count); elapsed time; memory footprint.

Not surprisingly, the last phase of the algorithm fails when using doubles: the outer hull computation, indeed, relies on the relative position of intersection points [13]. Hence, the time and memory evaluations are split in two parts, one regarding the algorithm without the outer hull computation, and one that includes this last phase. Quantitative results of this experiment are summarized in Table 1.

Table 1 reveals that the coding effort required to fully exploit the potential of the hybrid kernel is extremely limited. Indeed, with respect to the approximated version, the developer is just required to add an instruction at the beginning

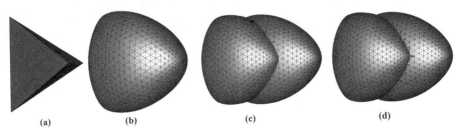

(a)   (b)   (c)   (d)

Fig. 1. The four phases of our test algorithm. An initial tetrahedron (a) is refined through five Loop subdivision steps (b). The resulting solid is duplicated, and one of the two copies is shifted along the X axis (c). The outer hull of the resulting two intersecting solids is computed (d).

Table 1. Quantitative comparison of three versions of the same algorithm showing the advantages of the hybrid approach proposed.

	Approximated	Exact	Hybrid
Num. code lines	2695	2701	2697
Time (no outer hull)	15 ms	81 ms	16 ms
Time (with outer hull)	n.a	2208 ms	413 ms
Memory (no outer hull)	9.2 MB	22.1 MB	9.9 MB
Memory (with outer hull)	n.a	58.4 MB	47.1 MB

(PM_Rational::$Kernel\_mode = approximated$) and one before the outer hull computation routine (PM_Rational::$Kernel\_mode = precise$). The additional code lines in the exact version of the test program are the various typedefs and kernel initializations needed by CGAL. Also, with respect to the approximated version, the increase in the elapsed time due to the use of PM_Rationals is negligible, whereas the need to check whether the approximated numbers would lead to unreliable results makes CGAL quite slower. Also, since the underlying *type* of PM_Rationals is double for the vast majority of the coordinates (i.e. all the vertices but those that represent intersection points), the memory footprint is not affected too much. Conversely, the use of CGAL's interval arithmetic has a much more significant impact in this sense due to the use of DAGs for all the points.

Similar experiments on more than a hundred mesh models demonstrate that, when there is no need to perform exact computations, using PM_Rationals instead of standard doubles slows the computation down of a factor of 8% on average. As far as the memory footprint is concerned, using PM_Rationals requires 12% more resources on average: this is mostly due to a typical behavior of compilers and of operating systems which allocate at least one byte for each class member. Thus, even if in principle 65 bits would be sufficient to encode a PM_Rational whose underlying *type* is double, 72 bits are used by the operating system due to such an alignment.

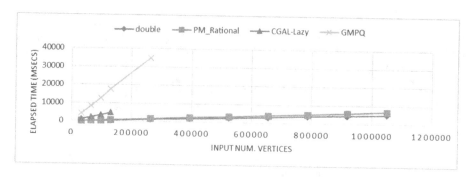

Fig. 2. Time necessary to perform a single Loop subdivision step. CGAL-based implementation crashes when the input exceeds 200 K vertices. This threshold is slightly higher for the GMPQ-based implementation.

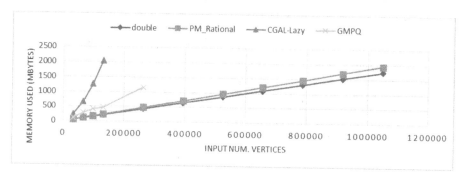

Fig. 3. Memory required to perform a single Loop subdivision step. CGAL-based implementation crashes when the input exceeds 200 K vertices. This threshold is slightly higher for the GMPQ-based implementation.

Analogous results were achieved during a further experiment where the program had to just perform a single Loop subdivision step on an input mesh made of N vertices. For this experiment, the same program was implemented using four different types to represent the coordinates: standard IEEE double precision FP numbers, PM_Rational, GMPQ, CGAL::Lazy_exact_nt<CGAL::Gmpq>. Figures 2 and 3 depict a comparison of the time and memory performances respectively as the number of input vertices increases. Note that the two versions based on GMPQ and CGAL fail much earlier as the input size grows.

4.1   Limitation

Non-rational numbers are not representable as PM_Rationals. Competing libraries such as, e.g., LEDA or CGAL, provide tools to represent a subset of these numbers: for example, algebraic numbers are somewhat useful in geometric computation and can be represented "symbolically" within LEDA. Unfortunately, this limitation for PM_Rationals is intrinsic and apparently can be solved only through an integration with a symbolic calculus module which would probably spoil the gain in performances. Hence, this is an open problem that represents an interesting direction for future research.

5 Summary and Conclusions

In this paper, the need for robust arithmetic in mesh processing algorithms has been re-casted to a novel paradigm where the user has a full control of the precision, in any part of the program and for any portion of the input dataset. Experiments demonstrated that this approach is more efficient than state-of-the-art solutions, in terms of both memory consumption and speed of the computation.

Clearly, the developer must know where and how to deal with robustness to fully exploit the potential of this new approach, but a specific algorithmic design is necessary in any case to guarantee robustness even with existing libraries (e.g. CGAL). Further research is still necessary to make development as easy as for traditional floating point arithmetic. A naive approach is to use the precise kernel for PM_Rationals everywhere, but this would make the program too slow in general. As an alternative, the developer may use as much precision as necessary just to make sure that ImatiSTL API functions return a correct result. In principle, the switch to the necessary precision level can be made automatically, but this makes sense only as long as the user is forced to use the provided API functions only. Unfortunately, preventing the user to insert custom PM_Rational operations would be probably a too strict constraint for a flexible development. A really effective solution to the problem would probably require an automated analysis of the source code.

Acknowledgements. This work has been partly supported by the international joint project on Mesh Repairing for 3D Printing Applications funded by Software Architects Inc (WA, USA). Thanks are due to the SMG members at IMATI for helpful discussions.

References

1. Shewchuk, J.R.: Lecture notes on geometric robustness. University of California at Berkeley (2013)
2. Shewchuk, J.R.: Adaptive precision floating-point arithmetic and fast robust geometric predicates. Discr. Comput. Geometry **18**, 305–363 (1997)
3. Visual Computing Lab: Vcglib: visualization and computer graphics library. http://vcg.sourceforge.net
4. RWTH: Openmesh: visualization and computer graphics library. http://www.openmesh.org/
5. Granlund, T.: The GNU multiple precision arithmetic library. TMG Datakonsult, Boston, MA, USA (1996)
6. Karamcheti, V., Li, C., Pechtchanski, I., Yap, C.: A core library for robust numeric and geometric computation. In: Proceedings of the Fifteenth Annual Symposium on Computational Geometry, pp. 351–359. ACM (1999)

7. Mehlhorn, K., Naher, S.: Leda: a platform for combinatorial and geometric computing. Commun. ACM **38**, 96–103 (1995)
8. Attene, M.: Direct repair of self-intersecting meshes. Graph. Models **76**, 658–668 (2014)
9. Pion, S., Fabri, A.: A generic lazy evaluation scheme for exact geometric computations. Sci. Comput. Program. **76**, 307–323 (2011)
10. Yap, C.: Robust geometric computation. In: Goodman, J.E., O'Rourke, J. (eds.) Handbook of Discrete and Computational Geometry, 2nd edn. CRC Press, LLC, Boca Raton (2004)
11. Goldberg, D.: What every computer scientist should know about floating-point arithmetic. ACM Comput. Surv. **23**, 5–48 (1991)
12. Loop, C.: Smooth subdivision surfaces based on triangles. Department of Mathematics, The University of Utah, Master Thesis (1987)
13. Campen, M., Attene, M., Kobbelt, L.: A practical guide to polygon mesh repairing. In: EUROGRAPHICS Tutorials, Eurographics, May 2012

Processing Large Geometric Datasets
in Distributed Environments

Daniela Cabiddu$^{(\boxtimes)}$ and Marco Attene

CNR-IMATI, Genova, Italy
{daniela.cabiddu,marco.attene}@ge.imati.cnr.it

Abstract. We describe an innovative Web-based platform to remotely perform complex geometry processing on large triangle meshes. A graphical user interface allows combining available algorithms to build complex pipelines that may also include conditional tasks and loops. The execution is managed by a central engine that delegates the computation to a distributed network of servers and handles the data transmission. The overall amount of data that is flowed through the net is kept within reasonable bounds thanks to an innovative mesh transfer protocol. A novel distributed divide-and-conquer approach enables parallel processing by partitioning the dataset into subparts to be delivered and handled by dedicated servers. Our approach can be used to process an arbitrarily large mesh represented either as a single large file or as a collection of files possibly stored on geographically scattered servers. To prove its effectiveness, we exploited our platform to implement a distributed simplification algorithm which exhibits a significant flexibility, scalability and speed.

Keywords: Distributed environments · Parallel computation · Geometry processing · Large meshes · Out-of-core

1 Introduction

In life science areas, several applications exist that allow remotely processing input data [38,40]. Such applications exploit the computational power of geographically scattered servers that communicate through traditional Internet connection. Each server exposes one or more remote services that can be invoked sequentially or in parallel to process a dataset received as an input.

This approach is scarcely considered in geometry processing literature where input datasets are easily made of millions of geometric elements and files encoding them may be larger than hundreds of gigabytes. Transferring these extremely large datasets on a distributed environment would slow the process down too much [6]. For this reason, geometry processing is usually performed by exploiting stand-alone tools and applications locally installed. When the main memory available on the local machine is not sufficient to load the input, divide and conquer approaches are used to subdivide the input into subparts, each of them

© Springer-Verlag GmbH Germany 2017
M.L. Gavrilova and C.J. Kenneth Tan (Eds.): Trans. on Comput. Sci. XXIX, LNCS 10220, pp. 97–120, 2017.
DOI: 10.1007/978-3-662-54563-8_6

sufficiently small to be processed [35]. Sometimes, multi-core technologies (e.g. GPUs) are exploited to process different subparts of the input simultaneously. Nevertheless, the memory shared among the concurrent processes imposes a sequentialization of I/O operations in any case.

Herewith, a Web-based platform is described to remotely run geometry processing workflows. The computational power of geographically distributed servers (i.e. processing nodes) is exploited to perform the actual computation. Our contribution is twofold: first, an optimized mesh transfer protocol is described that reduces the amount of data sent through the network and avoids possible bottlenecks; second, a divide-and-conquer approach is proposed that enables the possibility to run distributed parallel algorithms and guarantees efficiency. As a proof–of–concept, an innovative distributed mesh simplification algorithm is described that exploits our divide-and-conquer approach to distribute the computational load across multiple servers.

For the sake of simplicity, in the first part of the paper we assume that the input is stored as a single file on the disk of one of the servers. However, specific applications [4,17] acquire data from the real world and generate 3D models as collections of files, each representing a subpart of the whole. When such a collection is too large, it can be distributed on multiple machines. Although these datasets are natively partitioned, such a partition may not be compatible with the hardware limitations of the available processing nodes. In these cases, an input re-partitioning is required. In the second part of the paper (Sect. 6) we propose a novel approach to enable the possibility to run distributed parallel algorithms even on these extremely large data sets.

Summarizing, we propose an innovative approach to process arbitrary large geometric datasets. Thanks to our optimized transfer protocol and our divide-and-conquer method, well-known geometry processing workflows can be run efficiently on large datasets. To test our methods, a set of in-house Web services have been deployed on our servers and exploited. Each Web service is able to run a different geometric algorithm. Then, a former experimental phase has been focus on evaluate our mesh transfer protocol, while a second experimental phase has been focus on evaluating the distributed divide-and-conquer approach. Both experiments have been run a an heterogeneous dataset composed of meshes coming from public repositories [1,3] and from different research projects on processing large geometric datasets [2,4]. Both the computational time and the quality of the output meshes have been considered as a matter of comparison with the existing approaches. Our results demonstrate that distributed technologies can be actually exploited to efficiently run geometry processing even on extremely large datasets.

2   Related Work

Polygon meshes are the standard de-facto representation for 3D objects. A polygon mesh is a collection of polygons or "faces", that form the surface of the object. To describe a mesh, both geometric and topological information are required. The former includes the position of all the vertices, while the latter describes which vertices are connected to form edges and faces (i.e. triangles). While processing a mesh, either the geometry or the topology (or both) may be involved. Due to this complex structure, distributively processing meshes is a non-trivial task.

In the reminder, we focus on *triangle meshes*. This specific representation is used to describe objects coming from diverse industrial and research areas (e.g. design, geology, archaeology, medicine and entertainment).

2.1 Mesh Processing

Traditionally, mesh processing is performed by exploiting existing tools and applications that need to be installed on the local machine. Among them, MeshLab [11] and OpenFlipper [29] allow editing a mesh, saving the sequential list of executed operations and locally re-executing the workflow from their user interfaces. Pipelines can be shared in order to be rerun on different machines where the stand-alone applications need to be installed.

Campen and colleagues published WebBSP [8], an online service which allows to remotely run a few specific geometric operations. The user is required to select a single geometric algorithm from a set of available operations and upload an input mesh. Then, the algorithm is actually run on the server and a link to the output is sent to the user. Unfortunately, only a single operation can be run at each call and the service is accessible only from the WebBSP interface.

Geometric Web services were previously considered by Pitikakis [31] with the objective of defining semantic requirements to guarantee their interoperability. Though in Pitikakis's work Web services are stacked into hardcoded sequences, users are not allowed to dynamically construct workflows, and possible bottlenecks due to the transmission of large models are not dealt with.

Distributed parallelism has been exploited in [28,30] to provide both analysis and visualization tools. The possibility to exploit distributed parallelism for processing has been proposed in [32] but, due to the use of a distributed shared memory, the approach proposed is appropriate only on high-end clusters where local nodes are interconnected with particularly fast protocols.

2.2 Processing Large Polygon Meshes

Out-of-core approaches assume that the input does not need to be entirely loaded into main memory, and the computation operates on the loaded portion at each time [14,23,24,41]. Similarly, the external memory data structure proposed in [10] provides support for generic processing under the constraint of limited core memory. These methods are very elegant, but pre-processing operations required to pre-sort the input and generate the data structures require a significant time. Also, they are based on the idea of repeatedly loading parts of the input; thus, they are not suitable for distributed environments.

To speed up the computation, parallel approaches are often exploited [5,15,18,36]. Typically, a "master" processor partitions the input mesh and distributes the portions across different "slave" processors that perform the partial computations simultaneously. When all the portions are ready, the master merges the results together. The many slave processors available in modern GPU-based architectures are exploited in [34], while multi-core CPUs are exploited in [37]. Both methods are based on a memory shared among parallel processes to allow efficient communication. Distributed architectures are not provided with shared memory and, thus, different approaches are required to allow parallel processes to efficiently communicate. In [32], a hybrid architecture is described, where both shared and distributed memory are exploited. Parallel algorithms involving significant communication among processes can be implemented, but the communication costs will eventually limit the scaling.

Other effective out-of-core partitioning techniques are described in [25,26]. These methods typically require their input to come as a so-called "triangle soup", where the vertex coordinates are explicitly encoded for each single triangle. Since this representation is highly redundant, the most diffused formats (e.g. OFF, PLY, OBJ, ...) use a form of indexing, where vertex coordinates are encoded only once and each triangle refer to them through indexes. When the input is represented using an indexed format, it must be dereferenced using out-of-core techniques [9], but this additional step is time-consuming and requires significant storage resources. As an exception, the method proposed in [33] is able to work with indexed representations by relying on memory-mapped I/O managed by the operating system; however, if the face set is described without locality in the file, the same information is repeatedly read from disk and thrashing is likely to occur.

When the partial computations are comprehensively small enough to fit in memory, incore methods are exploited to merge the final result. To guarantee an exact contact among adjacent regions, slave processors are often required to keep the submesh boundary unchanged [36]. If necessary and if the final output is small enough, the quality of the generated mesh is enhanced by exploiting traditional incore algorithms in a final post-processing step. Differently, the external memory data structure [10] allows keeping the boundary consistent at each iteration. Depending on the specific type of geometric algorithm, different approaches may be exploited to guarantee boundary coherence. Vertex clustering is just an example used in mesh simplification [25]. Such a method has a cost in terms of output quality, when compared with more "adaptive" methods: the clustering distributes vertices uniformly on the surface, regardless the local morphology, hence tiny features are not guaranteed to be preserved.

3   The Web-Based Platform

The framework architecture is organized in three layers [21]: a graphical user interface that allows building new workflows from scratch, and uploading and invoking existing workflows; a set of Web services that wrap geometry processing tools; a workflow engine that handles the runtime execution by orchestrating the available Web services.

The Graphical User Interface. The graphical interface allows building geometric workflows and remotely running them on a selected input model. While building a new workflow, the user is asked to provide the list of geometry processing algorithms that constitute the pipeline, each to be selected from a list of available ones. Also, conditional tasks or loops can be defined. Once the whole procedure is ready, the user can turn it into an actual experiment by uploading an input mesh. If no input is associated, the workflow can be stored on the system as an "abstract" procedure that can be selected later for execution.

The Web Services. A Web service can be considered as a black box able to perform a specific operation on the mesh without the need of user interaction. A single server (i.e. a provider) can expose a plurality of Web services, each implementing a specific algorithm and identified by its own address. The system supports the invocation of two types of Web services, namely "atomic" and "boolean". An atomic service runs a simple operation on a mesh using possible input parameters, and produces another mesh as an output. Conversely, a boolean service just analyzes the mesh and returns a true/false value. Boolean Web services are used to support the execution of conditional tasks and loops.

Since input models may be stored on remote servers, we require that Web services are designed to receive the address of the input mesh and to download it locally; also, after the execution of the algorithm, the output must be made accessible through another address to be returned to the calling service.

The Workflow Engine. The workflow engine is the core of the system and orchestrates the invocation of the various algorithms involved. From the user interface it receives the specification of a geometry processing workflow and the address of an input mesh. The engine analyses the workflow, locates the most appropriate servers hosting the involved Web services, and sequentially invokes the various algorithms. For each operation, such a list of registered Web services is queried to retrieve which ones can perform the task, and the best performing one is selected [13] based on appropriate metadata to be provided upon registration of the service on our system. When the selected Web service is triggered for execution, it receives from the engine the address of the input mesh and possible parameters, runs its task and returns the address of the generated output to the engine. This latter information is sent to the next involved Web service as an input mesh or returned to the user interface when the workflow execution terminates.

4   Mesh Transfer Protocol

Not surprisingly, we have observed that the transfer of large-size meshes from a server to another according to the aforementioned protocol constitutes a bottleneck in the workflow execution, in particular when slow connections are involved.

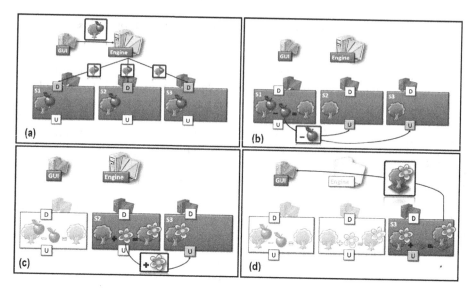

Fig. 1. Mesh transfer protocol example. The workflow is built by combining three operations. Thus, three servers are involved into the workflow execution. Each of them is able to download (D) meshes and update (U) the previously downloaded mesh by applying the corrections. (a) The address of the input mesh is broadcasted to all the involved servers that proceed with the download. (b) The first operation is run by the appropriate service that produces the corrections and returns the corresponding address to the engine. Such an address is shared in parallel to the successive servers, so that they can download the file and correct the prediction. (c) The second service runs the task and makes the correction available to allow the third server to update its local copy. (d) The last service is invoked to run the algorithm. The address of its output mesh is returned so that the user can directly download it.

Mesh compression techniques can be used to reduce the input size, but they do not solve the intrinsic problem [27]. In order to improve the transfer speed and thus efficiently support the processing of large meshes, we designed a mesh transfer protocol inspired on the prediction/correction metaphor used in data compression [39].

We have observed that there are numerous mesh processing algorithms that simply transform an input mesh into an output by computing and applying geometrical modifications. In all these cases it is possible to predict the result by assuming that it will be identical to the input, and it is reasonable to expect that the corrections to be transmitted can be more compactly encoded than the explicit result of the process.

The aforementioned observation can be exploited in our setting as shown in Fig. 1, where an example of execution of a simple workflow composed by three tasks is shown. Through the user interface, the user selects/sends a workflow and possibly the address of an input mesh to the workflow engine. The engine reads the workflow, searches for the available Web services, and sends in parallel to each of them the address of the input mesh. Each server is triggered to download the input model and save it locally. At the first step of the experiment, the workflow engine triggers the suitable Web service that runs the algorithm, produces the result, and locally stores the output mesh and the correction file (both compressed). Their addresses are returned to the workflow engine that forwards them to all the subsequent servers involved in the workflow. Each server downloads the correction and updates the local copy of the model according to it. Then, the workflow engine triggers the next service for which an up-to-date copy of the mesh is readily available on its local server. At the end of the workflow execution, the engine receives the address of the output produced by the last invoked Web service and returns it to the user interface, so that the user can download it.

In this scenario, the address of the input mesh is broadcasted to all the involved Web service once and Web services are able to download such a mesh simultaneously. Then, only correction files (which are sensibly smaller than the input mesh) travel through the network to allow each server to update its local copy of the mesh. In any case, each Web service produces both the correction and the actual result. When the correction is actually smaller than the results, this procedure produces significant benefits. Otherwise, the subsequent Web services can directly download the output instead of the corrections and no degradation is introduced. Note that lossless arithmetic coding is exploited by each Web service to compress either the output mesh or the correction file before making them travel the network.

5   Parallel Processing

Although our system theoretically allows processing any input mesh, remote servers have their own limitations and may not satisfy specific hardware requirements (eg. insufficient storage space, RAM, or computational performance) necessary to efficiently process large data. As a consequence, the remote server that is invoked may require a very long time to finish its task or, even worse, the process may be interrupted because of the insufficient main memory. In order to avoid these situations, the workflow engine is responsible for partitioning the input mesh into smaller subparts that can be elaborated by available processing services. When all the submeshes have been processed, they need to be merged to generate the final output. Both partitioning and merging operations are performed through out-of-core approaches. To allow final merging, an exact contact among adjacent regions must be guaranteed. Contrary to previous methods [36], our approach allows boundary modifications, while keeping the boundary consistent step by step.

For the sake of simplicity, our exposition assumes that all the servers have an equally-sized memory and comparable speed. Also, in the reminder of this section we describe the case where the input mesh is stored as a single input file. The treatment of pre-partitioned meshes whose parts are stored on different servers is described in Sect. 6.

5.1 Mesh Partitioning

We assume that the input mesh is encoded as an indexed mesh, since the most common file formats are based on this representation. Our mesh partitioning approach is mainly composed by the following sequential steps:

1. **Pre-Processing:** an initial binary space partition (BSP) is computed based on a representative vertex downsample;
2. **Vertex and Triangle Classification:** each vertex is assigned to the cell of the BSP where it falls, while each triangle is assigned to a selected BSP cell, based on the location of its vertices;
3. **Generation of independent sets:** each independent set includes submeshes that do not share any vertex, and thus they can be processed simultaneously;
4. **Optional post-processing:** depending on the specific geometry processing operation to be run by processing service.

Pre-processing. The mesh bounding box is computed by reading once the coordinates of all the input vertices. At the same time, a representative vertex down-sampling is computed and saved into main memory. Starting from the bounding box, an in-core binary space partition (BSP) is built by iteratively subdividing the cell with the greatest number of points. The root of the BSP refers to the whole downsampling. Each cell is split along its largest side. For each subdivision, each vertex in the parent cell is assigned to one of the two children according to its spatial location. If the vertex falls exactly on the splitting plane, it is assigned to the cell having the lowest barycenter in lexicographical order. The process is stopped when the number of vertices assigned to each BSP cell is at most equal to a given threshold, based on the number of vertices that each processing service is able to manage and the ratio between the number of input vertices and the downsample size.

Vertex and Triangle Classification. First, vertices are read one by one and assigned based on their spatial location as above. Some technical details are shown in Fig. 2.

Then, triangles are read one by one from T and assigned depending on their vertex position as follows:

– If at least two vertices belong to cell C_A, the triangle is assigned to cell C_A. In this case, if the third vertex belongs to a different cell C_B, a copy of the third vertex is added to C_A.
– If the three vertices belong to three different cells C_A, C_B, and C_C, the triangle is assigned to the cell having the smallest barycenter in lexicographical order (let it be C_A), and a copy of each vertex belonging to the other two cells is added to C_A.

At the end of the triangle classification, the BSP leaf cells represent a triangle-based partition of the input mesh geometry.

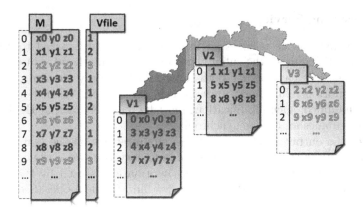

Fig. 2. Vertex classification. For each BSP cell, a corresponding file is created. Vertices are read one by one and assigned based on their spatial location. *Global* indexes are shown on the left of the original M, while *local* indexes are on the left of each V_i. For each vertex in M, both its global index and its coordinates are written on the corresponding V_i. V_{file} stores, for each vertex, the ID of the corresponding BSP cell. V_{file} is exploited during triangle classification to identify where the vertices of each triangle are located.

Independent Sets. An adjacency graph for the submeshes is defined where each node represents a BSP cell, and an arc exists between two nodes if their corresponding BSP cells are "mesh-adjacent". Two cells are considered to be mesh-adjacent if their corresponding submeshes share at least one vertex, that is, at least one triangle is intersected by the splitting plane between the two cells. Based on this observation, the adjacency graph is built during triangle classification and kept updated at each assignment. The problem of grouping together submeshes that are independent (e.g. no arc exists between the corresponding nodes) is solved by applying a greedy graph coloring algorithm [22]. Submeshes that belong to the same independent set can be processed simultaneously. Intuitively, the maximum number of nodes included in the same group is limited by the number of available processing services.

Post-processing. Depending on the specific geometric operation to be performed by processing services, some additional information from submesh's neighborhood may be required (e.g. the 1-ring neighborhood of boundary vertices is necessary to perform Laplacian smoothing). In these cases, a post-processing step is required to extract, for each submesh, the elements that constitute such a "support neighborhood". Such an information is then delivered to the processing service along with submesh to be processed.

5.2   Processing Services

Each processing service receives an input submesh and is asked to return an output mesh. If required, the submesh's support neighborhood is also provided. Processing services can modify both inner and boundary elements, while any possible support neighborhood must be kept unchanged. When boundary elements are modified, such modifications must be returned, so that the boundary of adjacent submeshes can be synchronized.

Besides the output mesh and possible modifications on the boundary, each processing service also encodes the list of boundary vertices of the output mesh into an additional file. Such a boundary information is used by the engine to efficiently merge the processed submeshes within a single model (Sect. 5.3).

Parallel Processing. When the same geometric operation is provided by more than one processing service, the engine exploits the generated independent sets to enable parallel processing. Each processing service is required to follow the rules described above. In the first iteration, each submesh in the current independent set is processed. Besides its output submesh, each processing service produces an additional file describing which modifications have been applied on the submesh boundary. This information is appended to adjacent submeshes and used a constraint during the next iterations (Fig. 3).

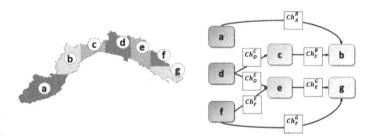

Fig. 3. Boundary synchronization. As an example, M_a and M_b are two neighbor submeshes. M_a is processed first. During the processing of M_a, all the changes introduced on the part of its boundary which is shared with M_b are stored in a file, namely Ch_b^a. When the turn of M_b comes, its processing service receives Ch_b^a and constrains M_b's boundary to change according to these instructions. Submeshes with the same color belong to the same independent set and can be processed simultaneously.

5.3   Output Merging

The engine is responsible for merging all the processed submeshes to generate a single indexed mesh. Mainly, the engine has two issues to deal with. First, vertices shared among two or more neighbor submeshes have to be identified and merged into a single point. Second, triplets of indexes representing triangles have to be rebuilt according to the final output indexing.

Since the final output may be too large to be loaded into main memory, an out-of-core merging method is proposed. As aforementioned, each processing service is also required to return the list of boundary vertices of the output mesh. Such a list is exploited to identify boundary vertices with no need to load the entire submesh. Algorithm 1 shows a more technical overview of our merging method.

Algorithm 1. Merge algorithm. n processed submeshes M'_i are merged into a single output M'. For each M'_i, the list of boundary vertices is stored in BV_i, encoded as a pair $\langle l, g \rangle$, where l is the local index and g the global index. Each BV_i is sorted by local index. An in-core map Map is used to store, for each boundary vertex already written to the final output, a mapping between its global index and its position in the merged mesh.

```
 1: procedure MERGE(M'_1, ..., M'_n, BV_1, ..., BV_n)
 2:     Create V_f and T_f files
 3:     Create empty Map
 4:     V_c ← 0                                          ▷ number of vertices added to final output
 5:     for each pair ⟨M'_i, BV'_i⟩ do
 6:         ⟨l, g⟩ ← first pair in BV_i
 7:         Allocate V(M'_i)                              ▷ an empty vector
 8:         for each v ∈ M'_i do
 9:             l_v ← local index of v
10:             if l_v ≠ l then                           ▷ v is an inner vertex
11:                 Write v coordinates in V_f
12:                 Append V_c to V(M'_i) and increment V_c
13:             else                                     ▷ v is a boundary vertex
14:                 f_v ← Map.find(g)
15:                 if g is not found then                ▷ v is not in V_f
16:                     Write v coordinates in V_f
17:                     Append V_c to V(M'_i)
18:                     Map.add(⟨g, V_c⟩) and increment V_c
19:                 else                                 ▷ v is already in V_f
20:                     V(M'_i)[l_v] ← f_v
21:                 ⟨l, g⟩ ← next pair in BV'_i
22:         for each t := (v_1, v_2, v_3) ∈ M'_i do
23:             Write V(M'_i)[v_1], V(M'_i)[v_2] and V(M'_i)[v_3] in T_f
24:     M' ← [header information] +V_f + T_f
25:     return M'
```

---

6   Distributed Input Dataset

When the input model is too large to be stored on a single machine, the mesh is stored as a distributed collection of files representing adjacent sections of the whole input model [4]. In this case, the engine may not have sufficient storage resources to download the whole input mesh on its own disk, and the existing sections of the model may not be compatible with the hardware limitations of the machines which host the processing services. Also, the final output may be too large to be stored on the engine's disk. Thus, a different approach is required to re-partition the input dataset (Fig. 4) and to generate the final output.

In principle, one could exploit the approach described in Sect. 5.1 to partition input submeshes which are too large, while the smallest ones can be processed as they are. Nevertheless, such an approach is inefficient when the number of small input submeshes is too large (i.e. because submeshes are unnecessarily small for the sake of processing). We propose an input repartitioning approach that maximizes the exploitation of available processing services.

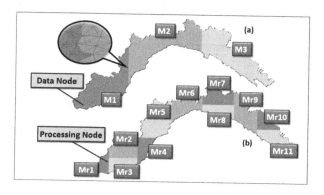

Fig. 4. Repartitioning. (a) The overall input mesh M. Each M_i is stored on a different data node. (b) Repartitioned M. M_j^rs with the same color are included in the same independent set.

Our reference scenario is shown in Fig. 5. The engine manages the input re-partitioning and the final output generation by delegating part of the computation to the data nodes. When the re-partitioning has been completed, a new collection of adjacent submeshes $\langle M_1^r, M_2^r, ..., M_m^r \rangle$ representing the original M is distributedly stored on the data nodes. The engine is responsible for grouping the generated submeshes into independent sets and for orchestrating the processing nodes to enable parallel processing. The result of each processing service is delivered back to the data node that hosts the input. It is worth noticing that, in this scenario, the engine works as an interface among data nodes and processing nodes. When a node is triggered for execution, it receives from the engine the address of the input data to be processed.

6.1   Input Repartitioning

The input repartitioning method is an extension of the the previously described approach (Sect. 5.1), where part of the computation is delegated to the data nodes.

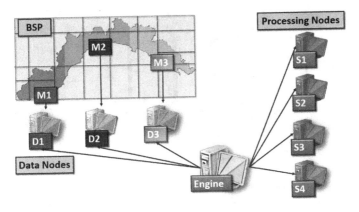

Fig. 5. Scenario. The original input mesh is defined as a collection of adjacent indexed submeshes $\langle M_1, M_2, M_3 \rangle$. Each M_i is stored on a different data node D_i. The engine manages the input re-partitioning and the final output generation by delegating part of the computation to the data nodes, while processing nodes are invoked for the actual computation.

Pre-processing. Each data node is required to compute both the bounding box and a representative vertex downsampling of its own original submesh. The engine exploits this information to build a BSP of the whole original mesh M. The BSP is stored on file to be distributed to the data nodes.

Vertex and Triangle Classification. Each data node assigns vertices and triangles of its original input portion to the corresponding BSP cell, according to their spatial location.

Generation of Independent Sets. The engine is responsible for building the adjacency graph for the generated submeshes and group them into independent sets. In some cases, a generated submesh may include portions of different original portion (e.g. M_2^r in Fig. 6). While building the independent sets, the engine is responsible to group together data coming from different data nodes and to send all of them to the same processing node.

6.2   Processing Services

When the input re-partitioning is completed, the dataset is ready to be processed. The engine is responsible of managing the actual processing by iteratively distributing each independent set to the available processing services. Note that processing services work as described in Sect. 5.2. Additionally, when a submesh is compose by portions coming from different data nodes (e.g. M_2^r in Fig. 6), a processing service is required to load all the portions into its main memory and merge them together before starting the actual computation. Since submeshes are guaranteed to be sufficiently small to be completely loaded, the merging

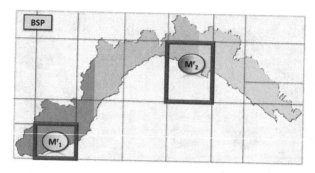

Fig. 6. The distributed BSP at the end of the repartitioning of $M = \langle M_1, M_2, M_3 \rangle$. As an example, M_1^r is a subpart of the original M_1 (red), while M_2^r is composed by two subparts of the original M_2 (green) and M_3 (yellow) respectively. (Color figure online)

operation is performed by an incore method. Consistently with the previous approach, each processing service generates an output mesh and an additional file listing its boundary vertices. Also, files storing the list of modifications applied on the submesh boundary are built and distributed to allow boundary synchronization among neighbor submeshes.

6.3 Distributed Output Merging

When all the submeshes have been processed by the available processing nodes, they should be merged to generate the final output. When the engine has not enough storage resources, the disk space of the data nodes is exploited. We assume that each data node has sufficient free storage resources to collectively store a final merged output.

Let D_i be the data node storing a set of generated submeshes. The outputs of the processing services responsible for their elaboration is returned to D_i, which is responsible for merging them into a single mesh by exploiting the previously described approach (Sect. 5.3) to perform the task. The final output is a distributed collection of processed submeshes, representing adjacent pieces of a huge mesh M', which is a modified version of the original M.

7   Mesh Simplification

The distributed simplification algorithm works as follows. In the first step, the engine partitions the mesh into a set of submeshes. Depending on the representation of the input dataset (distributed or not), one of the previously described algorithms (Sects. 5.1 or 6.1) is selected to perform the task. Generated submeshes are then grouped into independent sets. Each independent set is iteratively sent to the processing nodes for simplification. In the first iteration, each submesh is simplified in all its parts according to the target accuracy. Besides the simplified mesh, each processing service produces a set of additional files identifying which vertices on the submesh boundary were removed during simplification. Specifically, each file identifies vertices shared with a specific neighbor. When processing adjacent submeshes, this information is used as a constraint for their own simplification. When all the independent sets are processed, the final output is generated by joining the simplified submeshes along their boundaries, which are guaranteed to match exactly. If the engine has sufficient resources, the algorithm described in Sect. 5.3 is exploited. Otherwise, the approach described in Sect. 6.3 enables the possibility to distributedly store the final output.

Adaptivity. Each submesh is simplified by a single processing service through a standard iterative edge-collapse approach based on quadric error metric [19]. Every edge is assigned a "cost" that represents the geometric error introduced should it be collapsed. On each iteration, the lowest-cost edge is actually collapsed, and the costs of neighboring edges are updated. In order to preserve the appearance of the original shape, the simplification algorithm applied by each service stops when a maximum error max_E is reached. This approach provides an adaptively optimal result [7]. For each vertex, a quadric matrix is calculated without the need of any support neghborhood: if the vertex is on the submesh boundary, a partial quadric for boundaries [20] is calculated. To preserve the input topology, we constrain boundary vertices which are shared by more than two submeshes. By not simplifying these vertices, and by verifying the link condition for all the other vertices, we can guarantee that the resulting simplified submesh is topologically equivalent to the input.

Other Features. Our simplification algorithm proves the benefits provided by our partitioning/merging approach, but it also has other noticeable characteristics. Table 1 summarized the main features of such an algorithm and a comparison with the state of the art. However, their description would bring us too far from the scope of this paper, hence we refer the reader to [7] for details.

Table 1. Feature-based comparison with the state of the art.

	[26]	[36]	[5]	Ours
Out–Of–Core input	✓	✗	✓	✓
Out–of–Core output	✓	✗	✗	✓
Adaptivity	✗	✓	✓	✓
Distributable	✓	✓	✗	✓
Indexed mesh support	✗	✓	✓	✓

8   Results and Discussion

For the sake of experimentation, the proposed Workflow Engine has been deployed on a standard server running Windows 7, whereas other web services implementing atomic tasks have been deployed on different machines to constitute a distributed environment. However, since all the servers involved in our experiments were in the same lab with a gigabit network connection, we needed to simulate a long-distance network by artificially limiting the transfer bandwidth to 5 Mbps. All the machines involved in the experimentation are equipped with Windows 7 64bit, an Intel i7 3.5 GHz processor, 4 GB Ram and 1 T hard disk.

Then, to test such a system we defined multiple processing workflows involving the available web services. The dataset has been constructed by selecting some of the most complex meshes currently stored within the Digital Shape Workbench [3]. As an example, one of our test workflows is composed by the following operations: Removal of Smallest Components (RSC), Laplacian Smoothing (LS), Hole Filling (HF), and Removal of Degenerate Triangles (RDT). The same workflow was run on all the meshes in our dataset to better evaluate the performance gain achievable thanks to our concurrent mesh transfer protocol. Table 2 reports the size of the output mesh and the size of the correction file after each operation (both after compression) whereas Table 3 shows the total time spent by the workflow along with a more detailed timing for each single phase. As expected, the corrections related to tasks that locally modify the model (eg. RSC, HF, RDT) are significantly smaller than the whole output mesh by several orders of magnitude; corrections regarding more "global" tasks (eg. LS) are also smaller than the output mesh, although in this latter case the correction file is just two/three times smaller than the whole output. Nevertheless, these results confirm that the proposed concurrent mesh transfer protocol provides significant benefits when the single steps produce mainly little or local mesh changes.

For each mesh in our dataset, Table 3 shows the time required to be processed both in case the mesh transfer protocol is exploited (first line) or not (second line). Specifically, the time spent by each algorithm is reported in columns RSC, LS, HF, RDT, while columns $T_1 \ldots T_3$ and columns $U_1 \ldots U_3$ show the time needed to transfer the correction file to the subsequent Web service and the time spent to update the mesh by applying the correction respectively. For the sake of comparison, below each pair (T_i, U_i) we also included the time spent by transferring the whole compressed result instead of the correction file, and the overall relative gain achieved by our protocol is reported in the last column. It is worth noticing that, in all our test cases, the sum of the transfer and update times is smaller than the time needed to transfer the whole mesh, with a significant difference when the latter was produced by applying little local modifications on the input.

To test our partitioning and simplification algorithm, large meshes extracted from the Stanford online repository [1], from the Digital Michelangelo Project [2] and from the IQmulus Project [4] were used as inputs. Some small meshes have been included in our dataset to evaluate and compare the error generated by the part-by-part simplification.

For each input model, we ran several tests by varying the number of involved processing nodes and the maximum error threshold. We fixed the number N_v

Table 2. Output sizes (in KB). For each mesh and for each task, the first line shows the size of the compressed output mesh, while the second line reports the size of the compressed correction. Average compression ratio is 5:1. Acronyms indicate Removal of Smallest Components (RSC), Laplacian Smoothing (LS), Hole Filling (HF), and Removal of Degenerate Triangles (RDT). A modified version of the Hole Filling algorithm has been run to process "2.5D" geospatial data (*) in order to preserve their largest boundary.

Mesh	RSC	LS	HF	RDT
Rome*	14915	15551	14915	13166
	1	1425	1	1
Dolomiti*	11146	11637	11146	10588
	1	1402	1	1
Isidore	20573	23333	23717	25497
	11	9433	154	2
Nicolo	19498	21447	20601	20171
	3	9296	48	2
Neptune	39881	40131	39891	39937
	1	15237	1	1
Ramesses	17484	19544	19934	19802
	3	8754	149	3
Dancers	16457	18037	18325	18116
	1	7220	80	1

of vertices that should be assigned to each submesh to 1 M for very large input meshes. Table 4 shows the time spent by the system to finish the whole computation. The achieved speedup S_i is also shown, computed as $S_i = \frac{Time_1}{Time_i}$, where $Time_1$ is the sequential time and $Time_i$ is the time required to run the simplification on i servers. As expected, speedups are higher when the number of available processing nodes increases. More noticeably, speedup increases as the input size grows. Table in Fig. 7 reports the relation between the size of the input, and shows the time needed to partition it and the benefits provided by our re-partitioning algorithm. As a summarizing achievement, our method could partition the 25 GB OFF file representing the Atlas model ($\approx$0.5 billions triangles) in $\approx$25 min. As a matter of comparison, the engine's operating system takes more than 8 min to perform a simple local copy of the same file. Furthermore, the last experiment in Table 4 shows the time required to process the full-resolution Liguria model (1.1 Tb), represented as a collection of 10 indexed meshes stored on just as many data nodes. The repartitioning step requires less than 3 h. Note that more than 24 h would be required if the model is stored as a single OFF file on the engine hard disk.

To test the quality of output meshes produced by our algorithm, we used Metro [12] to measure the mean error between some small meshes and their

Table 3. Times (in seconds). Acronyms indicate Input Broadcast (**IB**), Removal of Smallest Components (**RSC**), Laplacian Smoothing (**LS**), Hole Filling (**HF**), and Removal of Degenerate Triangles (**RDT**). Cells labelled by T_i indicate the time needed to transfer the correction file. Cells labelled by U_i indicate the time needed to update the mesh by applying the correction. **Total** indicates the overall time required for the execution. **Benefits** indicates, for each experiment, how much the computation time decreases when our protocol is exploited. Computation times are reported both in case the mesh transfer protocol is exploited (upper line) and in case of "traditional" transfer (lower line). Note that a modified version of the Hole Filling algorithm has been run to process "2.5D" geospatial data (*) in order to preserve the largest boundary.

Mesh (# vertices)	IB	RSC	T_1	U_1	LS	T_2	U_2	HF	T_3	U_3	RDT	Total	Benefits
Rome* (957456)	20.4	5.8	0.0	0.0	8.4	2.3	9.4	5.5	0.0	0.0	6.9	58.7	104%
			23.9			24.9			23.9			119.7	
Dolomiti* (810000)	15.8	4.9	0.0	0.0	7.2	2.2	7.8	4.6	0.0	0.0	5.7	48.2	92%
			17.8			18.6			17.8			92.4	
Isidore (1071671)	33.0	7.7	0.0	5.8	12.4	15.1	7.1	8.4	0.2	6.0	13.8	109.5	67%
			32.9			37.3			37.9			183.4	
Nicolo (945924)	31.2	6.5	0.0	4.8	10.5	14.9	6.1	7.5	0.1	4.9	11.5	98.0	69%
			31.2			34.3			33.0			165.7	
Neptune (1321838)	63.8	13.0	0.0	0.0	18.6	24.4	11.0	12.6	0.0	0.0	14.4	157.8	99%
			63.8			64.2			63.8			314.2	
Ramesses (775715)	28.0	6.7	0.0	4.3	9.6	14.0	5.4	7.0	0.2	4.5	10.3	90.0	70%
			28.0			31.3			31.9			152.8	
Dancers (703207)	26.3	4.9	0.0	0.0	7.3	11.6	4.3	5.2	0.1	3.6	7.0	70.3	92%
			26.3			28.9			29.3			135.2	

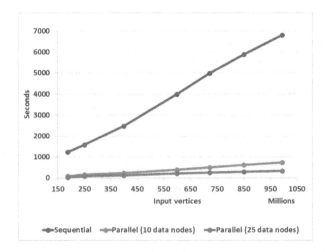

Fig. 7. Partitioning time vs input size: we can observe an approximately linear growth of the processing time as the input grows. When the input is pre-partitioned and scattered on different disks, the re-partitioning approach speeds up the input segmentation.

Table 4. Times (in seconds). Column labels: max_E is the threshold error (one thousandth of the bounding box diagonal of the input in all these experiments) expressed in absolute values, N_s is the number of available services, $\#ISs$ is the number of generated independent sets, while $\#V_o$ is the number of output vertices. Also, times are shown for each step: Partitioning (P), Simplification (S), and Merging (M). All the input meshes are stored as a single OFF file, except Liguria model (*) that is represented as a collection of 10 indexed meshes distributedly stored on 10 data nodes.

| Input | | | $\#ISs$ | $\#V_o$ | Times | | | | Speedup |
Mesh (# vertices)	max_E	N_s			P	S	M	Total	
Terrain (67873499)	0.00006	1	117	12166	497	302	1	800	–
		10	13	11697		64.45		562.45	1.42
		25	6	11660		13.37		511.37	1.56
St. Matthew (186836670)	3.01716	1	285	119121	1225.5	805.65	2.5	2033.65	–
		10	29	119035		104.05		1332.05	1.53
		25	13	119308		47.65		1275.65	1.59
Atlas (245837027)	3.35350	1	395	234084	1441	1481.25	4.5	2926.75	–
		10	42	234081		157.05		1602.55	1.83
		25	18	234091		72.95		1518.45	1.93
Liguria* (12986836670)	0.00006	1	26077	12174	9647	67278.60	1	76926.60	–
		10	3276	12144		8452.08		18100.08	4.25
		25	896	12153		2311.70		11959.70	6.42

simplifications. Results show that the number of services does not significantly affect the quality of the output. Unfortunately, Metro is based on an incore approach that evaluates the Hausdorff distance between the input mesh and the simplified one. Such an approach cannot be used to evaluate the quality of simplified meshes when the original version is too large. In these cases, quality can be assessed based on a visual inspection only. Figures 8, 9, and 10 show that high quality is preserved in any case and is not sensibly affected by the number of involved services.

8.1 Limitations

We enabled the possibility to analyze and process large geometric datasets. Nevertheless, some limitations should be taken into account when designing a parallel algorithm that exploits our divide-and-conquer method. First, our approach supports algorithms that modify the existing geometry, but does not consider the possibility to generate new geometric elements based on non strictly local information (e.g. hole filling). Second, processing services are assumed to perform local operations by analyzing at most a support neighborhood. Our divide-and-conquer approach is not suitable for processing services requiring global information. In this latter case, our proposal can be exploited only if an approximated result is accepted.

Nonetheless, for some specific global operations, our system can be easily customized and exploited as well. As an example, small components (e.g. those with low triangle counts) of the original input may be partitioned by the BSP. In this case, each processing service can just count the number of triangles of each

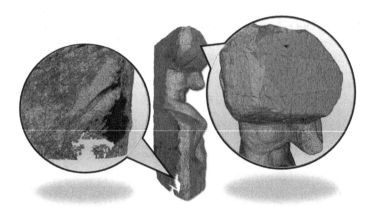

Fig. 8. Details of Atlas model simplified by exploiting 25 available services (original: ≈256 M vertices, simplified: ≈234 K vertices)

Fig. 9. Detail of simplified Terrain model (original: ≈68 M vertices, simplified: ≈115 K vertices). Nearly high fields are naturally supported

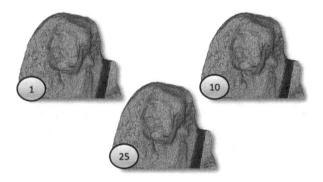

Fig. 10. Detail of St Matthew model simplified by 1, 10, and 25 servers (original: ≈187 M vertices, simplified: ≈1195 K vertices)

component which is connected in the submesh. Such an information is returned to the engine that, thanks to the BSP adjacency graph, can sum the partial counts for adjacent sub-components without the need to explicitly load mesh elements in memory. Thus, the engine can identify the smallest components and tell the services to remove them in a second iteration.

9   Conclusions

We proposed a workflow-based framework to support collaborative research in geometry processing. The platform is accessible from any operating system through a standard Web browser with no hardware or software requirements. A prototypal version is available at http://visionair.ge.imati.cnr.it/workflows/. Scientists are allowed to remotely run geometric algorithms provided by other researchers as Web services and to combine them to create executable geometric workflows. No specific knowledge in geometric modelling and programming languages is required to exploit the system.

As an additional advantage, short-lasting experiments can be re-executed on the fly when needed and there is no more need to keep output results explicitly stored on online repositories. Since experiments can be efficiently encoded as a list of operations, sharing them instead of output models sensibly reduces required storage resources. The architecture is open and fully extensible by simply publishing a new algorithm as a Web service and by communicating its URL to the system. Moreover, we have demonstrated that the computing power of a network of PCs can be exploited to significantly speedup the processing of large triangle meshes and we have shown that the overhead due to the data transmission is much lower than the gain in speed provided by parallel processing.

In its current form, our system has still a few weaknesses. First, experiments can be reproduced only as long as the involved Web services are available and are not modified by their providers. To reduce the possibility of workflow decay [42] a certain level of redundancy would be required. Second, our system does not allow to execute semi-automatic pipelines, that is with user interaction. Such a functionality would require the engine to interrupt the execution waiting for the user intervention.

Several future directions are possible, both in terms of improvement of the platform capabilities and enrichment of the geometry processing operations. One of the objectives of our future research is to simplify the work of potential contributor by enabling the engine to automatically compute the list of editing operations. A possible solution may be inspired on [16], even if the high computational complexity of this method would probably hinder our gain in speed.

Acknowledgements. This work is partly supported by the EU FP7 Project no. ICT–2011-318787 (IQmulus) and by the international joint project on Mesh Repairing for 3D Printing Applications funded by Software Architects Inc (WA, USA). The authors are grateful to all the colleagues at IMATI for the helpful discussions.

References

1. The Stanford 3D Scanning Repository (1996)
2. The Digital Michelangelo Project (2009)
3. DSW v5.0 - visualization virtual services (2012)
4. Iqmulus: A High-volume Fusion and Analysis Platform for Geospatial Point Clouds, Coverages and Volumetric Data Sets (2013)
5. Brodsky, D., Pedersen, J.B.: Parallel model simplification of very large polygonal meshes. In: Proceedings of Parallel and Distributed Processing Techniques and Applications (PDPTA 2002), vol. 3, pp. 1207–1215 (2002)
6. Cabiddu, D., Attene, M.: Distributed processing of large polygon meshes. In: Proceedings of Smart Tools and Apps for Graphics (STAG 2015) (2015)
7. Cabiddu, D., Attene, M.: Large mesh simplification for distributed environments. Comput. Graph. **51**, 81–89 (2015)
8. Campen, M.: WebBSP 0.3 beta (2010). http://www.graphics.rwth-aachen.de/webbsp
9. Chiang, Y.J., Silva, C.T., Schroeder, W.J.: Interactive out-of-core isosurface extraction. In: IEEE Visualization 1998, pp. 167–174 (1998)
10. Cignoni, P., Montani, C., Rocchini, C., Scopigno, R.: External memory management and simplification of huge meshes. IEEE Trans. Vis. Comput. Graph. **9**(4), 525–537 (2003)
11. Cignoni, P., Corsini, M., Ranzuglia, G.: Meshlab: an open-source 3d mesh processing system. ERCIM News **73**, 45–46 (2008)
12. Cignoni, P., Rocchini, C., Scopigno, R.: Metro: measuring error on simplified surfaces. Comput. Graph. Forum **17**(2), 167–174 (1998)
13. Claro, D.B., Albers, P., Hao, J.: Selecting web services for optimal composition. In: Proceedings of the 2nd International Workshop on Semantic and Dynamic Web Processes (SDWP 2005), pp. 32–45 (2005)
14. Cuccuru, G., Gobbetti, E., Marton, F., Pajarola, R., Pintus, R.: Fast low-memory streaming MLS reconstruction of point-sampled surfaces. In: Proceedings of Graphics Interface, GI 2009, pp. 15–22. Canadian Information Processing Society, Toronto (2009)
15. Dehne, F., Langis, C., Roth, G.: Mesh simplification in parallel. In: Proceedings of Algorithms and Architectures for Parallel Processing (ICA3P 2000), pp. 281–290 (2000)
16. Denning, J.D., Pellacini, F.: Meshgit: diffing and merging meshes for polygonal modeling. ACM Trans. Graph **32**(4), 35: 1–35: 10 (2013)
17. Farr, T.G., Rosen, P.A., Caro, E., Crippen, R., Duren, R., Hensley, S., Kobrick, M., Paller, M., Rodriguez, E., Roth, L., Seal, D., Shaffer, S., Shimada, J., Umland, J., Werner, M., Oskin, M., Burbank, D., Alsdorf, D.: The shuttle radar topography mission. Rev. Geophys. **45**(2), RG2004 (2007)
18. Franc, M., Skala, V.: Parallel triangular mesh reduction. In: Proceedings of Scientific Computing, ALGORITMY 2000, pp. 357–367 (2000)
19. Garland, M., Heckbert, P.S.: Surface simplification using quadric error metrics. In: Proceedings of SIGGRAPH 1997, pp. 209–216 (1997)
20. Heckbert, P.S., Garland, M.: Optimal triangulation and quadric-based surface simplification. J. Comput. Geometry Theory Appl. **14**(1–3), 49–65 (1999)
21. Hollingsworth, D.: Workflow management coalition - the workflow reference model. Technical report, January 1995

22. Hutter, M., Knuth, M., Kuijper, A.: Mesh partitioning for parallel garment simulation. In: Proceedings of WSCG 2014, pp. 125–133 (2014)
23. Isenburg, M., Lindstrom, P.: Streaming meshes. In: Visualization (VIS 2005), pp. 231–238. IEEE, October 2005
24. Isenburg, M., Lindstrom, P., Gumhold, S., Snoeyink, J.: Large mesh simplification using processing sequences. In: Visualization (VIS 2003), pp. 465–472, October 2003
25. Lindstrom, P.: Out-of-core simplification of large polygonal models. In: Proceedings of SIGGRAPH 2000, pp. 259–262 (2000)
26. Lindstrom, P., Silva, C.T.: A memory insensitive technique for large model simplification. In: IEEE Visualization, pp. 121–126 (2001)
27. Maglo, A., Lavoué, G., Dupont, F., Hudelot, C.: 3d mesh compression: survey, comparisons, and emerging trends. ACM Comput. Surv. 47(3), 44: 1–44: 41 (2015)
28. Meredith, J.S., Ahern, S., Pugmire, D., Sisneros, R.: EAVL: the extreme-scale analysis and visualization library. In: Eurographics Symposium on Parallel Graphics and Visualization. The Eurographics Association (2012)
29. Möbius, J., Kobbelt, L.: OpenFlipper: an open source geometry processing and rendering framework. In: Boissonnat, J.-D., Chenin, P., Cohen, A., Gout, C., Lyche, T., Mazure, M.-L., Schumaker, L. (eds.) Curves and Surfaces 2010. LNCS, vol. 6920, pp. 488–500. Springer, Heidelberg (2012). doi:10.1007/978-3-642-27413-8_31
30. Moreland, K., Ayachit, U., Geveci, B., Ma, K.L.: Dax toolkit: a proposed framework for data analysis and visualization at extreme scale. In: IEEE Symposium on Large Data Analysis and Visualization (LDAV 2011), pp. 97–104 (2011)
31. Pitikakis, M.: A semantic based approach for knowledge management, discovery and service composition applied to 3D scientif objects. Ph.D. thesis, University of Thessaly, School of Engineering, Department of Computer and Communication Engineering (2010)
32. C. Sewell, Lo, L.T., Ahrens, J.: Portable data-parallel visualization and analysis in distributed memory environments. In: IEEE Symposium on Large-Scale Data Analysis and Visualization (LDAV 2013), pp. 25–33 (2013)
33. Shaffer, E., Garland, M.: Efficient adaptive simplification of massive meshes. In: Proceedings of Visualization 2001, pp. 127–134 (2001)
34. Shontz, S.M., Nistor, D.M.: CPU-GPU algorithms for triangular surface mesh simplification. In: Jiao, X., Weil, J.-C. (eds.) Proceedings of the 21st International Meshing Roundtable, pp. 475–492. Springer, Heidelberg (2013)
35. Silva, C., Chiang, Y., Corra, W., El-sana, J., Lindstrom, P.: Out-of-core algorithms for scientific visualization and computer graphics. In: Visualization 2002 Course Notes (2002)
36. Tang, X., Jia, S., Li, B.: Simplification algorithm for large polygonal model in distributed environment. In: Huang, D.-S., Heutte, L., Loog, M. (eds.) ICIC 2007. LNCS, vol. 4681, pp. 960–969. Springer, Heidelberg (2007). doi:10.1007/978-3-540-74171-8_97
37. Thomaszewski, B., Pabst, S., Blochinger, W.: Parallel techniques for physically based simulation on multi-core processor architectures. Comput. Graph. 32(1), 25–40 (2008)
38. Tiwari, A., Sekhar, A.K.T.: Workflow based framework for life science informatics. Comput. Biol. Chem. 31(56), 305–319 (2007)
39. Touma, C., Gotsman, C.: Triangle mesh compression. In: Graphics Interface, pp. 26–34 (1998)

40. Wolstencroft, K., Haines, R., Fellows, D., Williams, A., Withers, D., Owen, S., Soiland-Reyes, S., Dunlop, I., Nenadic, A., Fisher, P., Bhagat, J., Belhajjame, K., Bacall, F., Hardisty, A., Nieva de la Hidalga, A., Balcazar Vargas, M.P., Sufi, S., Goble, C.: The Taverna workflow suite: designing and executing workflows of web services on the desktop, web or in the cloud. Nucl. Acids Res. **41**(Web Server issue), gkt328–W561 (2013)

41. Jianhua, W., Kobbelt, L.: A stream algorithm for the decimation of massive meshes. In: Proceedings of the Graphics Interface 2003 Conference, Halifax, Nova Scotia, Canada, pp. 185–192, June 2003

42. Zhao, J., Gomez-Perez, J.M., Belhajjame, K., Klyne, G., Garcia-cuesta, E., Garrido, A., Hettne, K., Roos, M., De Roure, D., Goble, C.: Why workflows break: understanding and combating decay in Taverna workflows, pp. 1–9 (2012)

Decision Fusion for Classification of Content Based Image Data

Rik Das[1(✉)], Sudeep Thepade[2], and Saurav Ghosh[3]

[1] Department of Information Technology, Xavier Institute of Social Service,
Ranchi, Jharkhand, India
rikdas78@gmail.com
[2] Department of Information Technology,
Pimpri Chinchwad College of Engineering, Pune, India
sudeepthepade@gmail.com
[3] A.K. Choudhury School of Information Technology,
University of Calcutta, Kolkata, West Bengal, India
sauravghoshcu@gmail.com

Abstract. Information recognition by means of content based image identification has emerged as a prospective alternative to recognize semantically analogous images from huge image repositories. Critical success factor for content based recognition process has been reliant on efficient feature vector extraction from images. The paper has introduced two novel techniques of feature extraction based on image binarization and Vector Quantization respectively. The techniques were implemented to extract feature vectors from three public datasets namely Wang dataset, Oliva and Torralba (OT-Scene) dataset and Corel dataset comprising of 14,488 images on the whole. The classification decisions with multi domain features were standardized with Z score normalization for fusion based identification approach. Average increase of 30.71% and 28.78% in precision were observed for classification and retrieval respectively when the proposed methodology was compared to state-of-the art techniques.

Keywords: Binarization · Fusion · Image classification · Image retrieval · Query classification · t test · Vector quantization

1 Introduction

A rapid enhancement in collections of digital images has been observed in recent years. Image data has been generated in gigabytes as a rich source of information with the evolution of internet and high end image capturing devices [1, 2]. Traditionally, manual annotation of images has been considered as the standard technique to identify the image data from the databases. The task has become gradually impossible in contemporary scenario with plethora of digital libraries being incorporated with each passing day. Irrelevant classification results can be generated in majority as the images were named based on individual user perceptions which may vary on case to case basis. Content based image recognition has emerged as a fruitful alternative to manage the wealthy foundation of image information by means of image classification and retrieval

© Springer-Verlag GmbH Germany 2017
M.L. Gavrilova and C.J. Kenneth Tan (Eds.): Trans. on Comput. Sci. XXIX, LNCS 10220, pp. 121–138, 2017.
DOI: 10.1007/978-3-662-54563-8_7

[3]. The process of content based image identification has been largely dependent on feature extraction techniques [4]. The existing techniques have resulted in extraction of feature vectors with huge dimensions. This has resulted in increased training time for the classifiers which has made the classification process invariably slow. On the other hand, an image has diverse set of features in it which can hardly be explored by means of a single feature extraction technique [5]. Hence, the authors have proposed two different feature extraction techniques based on binarization and Vector Quantization respectively. The research objectives have been enlisted as follows:

- Reducing the dimension of feature vectors
- Successfully implementing fusion based method of content based image identification
- Statistical validation of research results
- Comparison of research results with state-of-the art techniques

The techniques were implemented on three different public datasets namely, Wang dataset, Oliva and Torralba (OT-Scene) dataset and Corel dataset respectively which comprised of 14,488 images on the whole. The classification decisions with the individual techniques were fused by means of Z score normalization to formulate a fusion based classification model. Further, retrieval architecture with classified query was introduced to evaluate the retrieval efficiency with the proposed techniques. The precision values have shown an average increase of 30.71% and 28.78% for classification and retrieval results respectively when compared to the state-of-the art techniques. The findings were statistically validated with a paired t test [6].

2 Related Work

Binarization and Vector Quantization have been readily utilized by the existing feature extraction techniques for proficient signature extraction from images. The popularity of the techniques was facilitated by the relatively simple structure and computation. Binarization of images has been categorized into three different methods of threshold selection namely mean threshold selection, local threshold selection and global threshold selection. Mean threshold technique for binarization was used for capturing significant information as features from bit planes of images as well as from fusion of generic and flipped image varieties [7, 8] for better classification results. Ternary mean threshold [9] and multilevel mean threshold [10] for binarization has also assisted the extraction of substantial features for image identification. Nevertheless, standard deviation of the gray values has not been considered in the aforesaid techniques to understand the spread of data. Traditional global threshold selection technique using Otsu's method [11, 12] is based on image variance. Application of local threshold selection techniques in contemporary researches for feature extraction has exhibited the use of image variance and contrast as factors for image binarization [13–19]. Image features has been well represented by codebook generation in the past by means of Vector Quantization [20]. Vector Quantization (VQ) has diverse categories including classified VQ, address VQ, finite state VQ, side match VQ, mean-removed classified VQ, and predictive classified VQ [21–26]. Designing of codebook using Vector

Quantization techniques has assisted in boosting up the performance of image identification. Image identification with reduced space complexity has achieved higher retrieval by utilizing genetic algorithm to obtain the most favourable boundaries of the numerical variables [27]. A novel geometric verification scheme named DT RANSAC has been discussed in [43] which has revealed better retrieval results compared to existing techniques. Color moments and moments on Gabor filter responses were used to calculate local descriptors of color and texture to facilitate retrieval [28]. Fuzzy set theoretic approach has been explored to extract visually significant point features images for efficient recognition [29]. In [30], improved retrieval accuracy was observed by combining color layout descriptor and Gabor texture descriptor. Image signatures were designed with color, texture and spatial structure descriptors [31]. Neural network architecture has been initiated for image identification using wavelet packets and Eigen values of Gabor filters feature extraction techniques [32]. A technique for retrieval has been devised on intra-class and inter-class features in [33]. A modified color motif co-occurrence matrix (MCMCM) has been proposed for content-based image retrieval [34]. In [35], fusion of Edge Histogram Descriptor (EHD) and Angular Radial Transform (ART) technique has been proposed, which has shown significant improvement for image retrieval in hybrid environment. The authors have identified a common drawback in majority of the discussed techniques in the literature. The dimension of the extracted feature vectors is of the size of the image which produces hefty image signatures. This, in turn, increases the computational overhead. The authors have proposed two different feature extraction techniques in which the size of the feature vector is considerably small and independent of the image dimension. The results of image recognition with the proposed techniques have outperformed the state-of-the art techniques.

3   Proposed Techniques

Two different techniques namely feature extraction with image binarization and feature extraction with vector quantization have been proposed for multi-technique feature extraction from the image dataset. The proposed techniques have considered extraction of feature vectors in three different color spaces. Let the total number of gray levels present in the image be G. Threshold selection has taken linear time $O(G)$ for all the gray levels. Number of color components was 3. Let the number of gray level in each color component be N. Total number of iteration required was $O(3N)$. Thus the time complexity of the proposed method was linear.

Each of the techniques has been enlisted in the following subsections.

3.1   Feature Extraction with Image Binarization

Binarization technique differentiates the image into foreground and background pixel classes. This has been beneficial to identify the object of interest in the foreground class. Primarily, three different color components namely, Red (R), Green (G) and Blue (B) are extracted from the images. Each component is binarized with Bernsen's local adaptive technique of threshold selection based on contrast of an image. The Bernsen algorithm has considered each pixel (i, j) surrounded by a square window of recommended window size $w = 31$ [15]. The threshold is calculated as a midrange value, denoted by the mean of the minimum gray value $G_{low}(i, j)$ and maximum gray value $G_{high}(i, j)$ within a suggested local window. Threshold $Th(i, j)$ within the local window is computed as in Eq. 1.

$$Th(i, j) = 0.5\{\max w[I(i+m, j+n)] + \min w[I(i+m, j+n)]\} \tag{1}$$

when, contrast $C(i,j) = G_{high}(i, j) - G_{low}(i,j) \geq 15$.

A pixel within the window is designated as background or foreground pixel of the image according to the class that most suitably portrayed the window when the computed value of contrast $C(i, j)$ in Eq. 2 was less than a certain contrast threshold k (usually for images of global contrast 255 the threshold value has been set as 15).

$$C(i,j) = G_{high}(i, j) - G_{low}(i,j) \tag{2}$$

The algorithm has been largely dependent on the value of k and the size of the window. The binarization process has been illustrated in Fig. 1. The foreground pixel values designated with 1 in the binarized images are grouped into higher intensity cluster and the background pixel values denoted by 0 are grouped into lower intensity cluster. The authors have reduced the feature size by considering the mean and standard deviation of each group and added together for individual groups to form two feature vectors for each color component as in Eqs. 3–8. Thus, 6 feature vectors are calculated for each image using the binarization method. In case of binarization with conventional Bernsen's method, the feature size after binarization becomes equal to the size of the image as each of the foreground pixels has been denoted by 1 and background as 0. But, in our method we have drastically reduced the feature size to 6 on the whole irrespective of the image dimension.

$$xhi_{mean} = mean \sum_{p} \sum_{q} (x(p,q)) > Tx \tag{3}$$

$$xhi_{stdev} = \sigma \sum_{p} \sum_{q} (x(p,q)) > Tx \tag{4}$$

$$xhi_{F.V.} = xhi_{mean} + (xhi_{mean} + xhi_{stdev}). \tag{5}$$

$$xlo_{mean} = mean \sum_{p} \sum_{q} (x(p,q)) < Tx \tag{6}$$

$$xlo_{stdev} = \sigma \sum_{p} \sum_{q} (x(p,q)) < Tx \tag{7}$$

$$xlo_{F.V.} = xlo_{mean} + (xlo_{mean} + xlo_{stdev}) \tag{8}$$

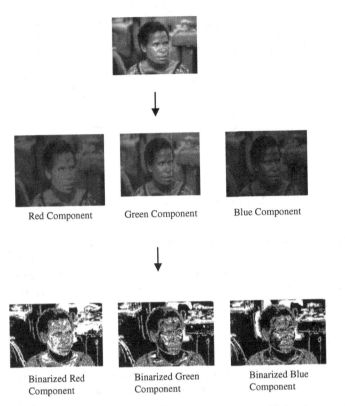

Fig. 1. Binarization with Bernsen's local threshold selection (Color figure online)

3.2 Feature Extraction with Vector Quantization

Feature extraction can be done from the spatial arrangements of color or intensities with the help of texture analysis. Same histogram distribution can have different texture representation, which can act as a tool for extraction of distinct features. Vector Quantization has been used to generate codebook as feature vectors from the images. A k dimensional Euclidian space is mapped by means of Vector Quantization into a finite subset. The codebook is represented by the finite set CB as in Eq. 9.

$$CB = \{Ci/i = 1, 2, \ldots, N\} \qquad (9)$$

where, $Ci = (ci1, ci2, \ldots, cik)$ is a codevector
N is the size of codebook

The authors have followed Linde - Buzo - Gray (LBG) algorithm for generation of codevectors in which the images are divided into non overlapping blocks which were converted to training vector $Xi = (xi1, xi2, \ldots\ldots, xik)$ [41]. The training set is formed with each training vector of dimension 12 comprising of Red (R), Green (G) and Blue (B) components of 2×2 neighbouring pixels. Further, the first code vector is calculated by computing the centroid of the entire training set. The process is followed by generation of two trial code vectors $v1$ and $v2$ by adding and subtracting constant error

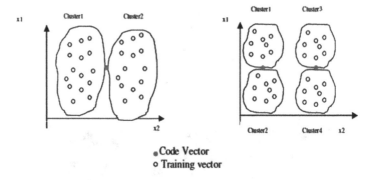

Fig. 2. Clustering process for codebook generation

to the centroid. The closeness of each training vector is determined to the trial vectors and two clusters are created based on proximity of the training vectors to $v1$ and $v2$ as in Fig. 2. Two centroids are calculated from the two newly formed clusters to produce two code vectors for a codebook of size 2. The aforesaid process is repeated with the centroids to generate desired size of codebook which is 16 in this case.

4 Matching

The image similarity measures have been determined by evaluating distance between set of image features and higher similarity has been characterized by shorter distance [37]. The distance between query image Q and database image T is calculated with City block distance and Euclidian distance for binarization and vector quantization techniques of feature extraction respectively as in Eqs. 10 and 11.

$$D_{cityblock} = \sum_{i-1}^{n} |Q_i - D_i| \tag{10}$$

$$D_{euclidian} = \sqrt{\sum_{i=1}^{n} (Q_i - D_i)^2} \tag{11}$$

where, Q_i is the query image and D_i is the database image.

The calculated distances for the individual techniques are standardized by Z score normalization based on mean and standard deviation of the computed values as in Eq. 12. In general, a feature vector with higher values of attributes tends to have greater effect or "weight." Hence, to avoid dependence on the choice of feature values of different feature vectors from diverse techniques, the data should be normalized or standardized. This has transformed the data to fall within a common range such as [–1, 1] or [0.0, 1.0]. Normalizing the data has attempted to provide all the feature vector extraction process with equal weights.

$$dist_n = \frac{dist_i - \mu}{\sigma} \tag{12}$$

where, μ is the mean and σ is the standard deviation

Henceforth, the distances are amalgamated as the weighted sum of the distances of the individual techniques. Calculation of weights is carried out form the individual

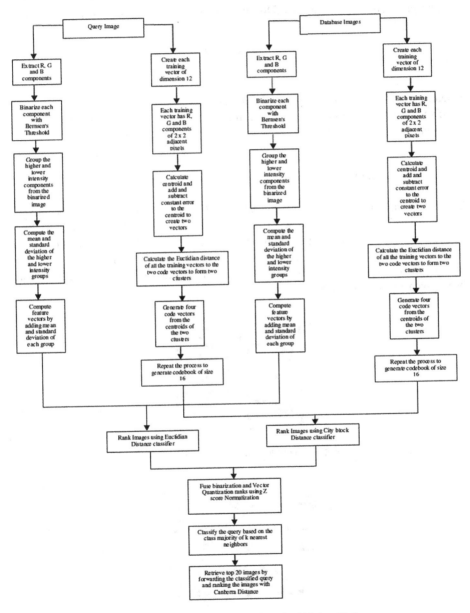

Fig. 3. Fusion framework for retrieval with classified query

average precision of each technique. Finally, the image is classified based on the class majority of k nearest neighbors [36] where value of k is

$$k \leq \sqrt{number..of..training..instances}$$

The classified image is forwarded for retrieval purpose. The image is a classified query and has searched for similar images only within the class of interest. Ranking of the images is done with Canberra Distance measure as in Eq. 13 and top 20 images were retrieved.

$$D_{canberra} = \sum_{i=1}^{n} \frac{|Q_i - D_i|}{|Q_i| + |D_i|} \tag{13}$$

where, Q_i is the query image and D_i is the database image.

The process of fusion based classification and then retrieval with classified query has been illustrated in Fig. 3.

5   Datasets Used

Three different datasets namely Wang dataset (10 different categories of 1000 images of dimension 256 × 384 or 384 × 256), Oliva and Torralba (OT-Scene) dataset (2688 images and is divided into eight different categories) and Corel dataset (10,800 images with 80 different categories of images of dimension 80 × 120 or 120 × 80) has been used for the classification purpose [38–40]. A sample collage of each of the datasets has been given in Figs. 4, 5 and 6.

Fig. 4. Sample collage for Wang dataset

Fig. 5. Sample collage for OT-Scene dataset

Fig. 6. Sample collage for Corel dataset

6 Results and Discussions

The research has been conducted using Matlab version 7.11.0(R2010b) installed in a system having Intel core i5 processor with 4 GB RAM under Microsoft Windows environment. At the outset, the precision and recall values for classification are determined on three different public datasets namely, Wang dataset, OT scene dataset and Corel dataset. Further, the precision, recall and F1 Score values of the fused architecture for classification are compared against state-of-the art techniques. The precision, recall and F1 Score are represented by Eqs. 14–16.

$$Precision = \frac{TP}{TP + FP} \tag{14}$$

$$TPRate/Recall = \frac{TP}{TP + FN} \tag{15}$$

$$F1score = \frac{2 * Precision * Recall}{Precision + Recall} \tag{16}$$

True Positive (TP) = Number of instances classified correctly
True Negative (TN) = Number of negative results created for negative instances
False Positive (FP) = Number of erroneous results as positive results for negative instances
False Negative (FN) = Number of erroneous results as negative results for positive instances

Subsequent precision and recall values for classification using two different techniques of feature extraction have been given in Figs. 7 and 8.

The precision and recall values shown in Figs. 7 and 8 has indicated higher classification accuracy by feature extraction with Vector Quantization compared to feature extraction with binarization in all the three datasets namely Wang dataset, OT Scene dataset and Corel dataset.

Henceforth, a statistical technique named Z score normalization has been implemented to fuse the classification decision with two different techniques of feature extraction. The fusion technique is carried out with Wang dataset. The results of classification with decision fusion has shown 93% precision and 92% recall which has clearly outperformed the precision and recall values obtained with individual feature

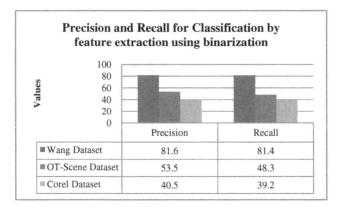

Fig. 7. Precision and recall for classification by feature extraction with binarization

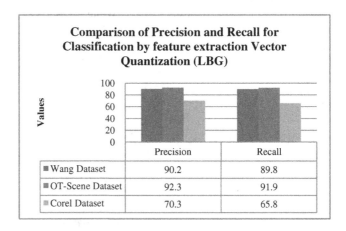

Fig. 8. Precision and recall for classification by feature extraction with vector quantization

extraction techniques. Further, the precision, recall and F1 Score values obtained by classification decision fusion are compared to state-of-the art techniques. The comparison has been accomplished with Wang dataset as in Fig. 9. The comparison of average Precision, Recall, F1 Score and MR curves of various techniques has been given in Fig. 10.

It is observed that the proposed architecture of classification has outperformed all the contemporary techniques discussed in the literature as in Fig. 9.

A paired t-test (2 tailed) is performed to compute the p-values for the precision for classification with the existing techniques with respect to the proposed technique. The actual difference between the two means for variation in precision results of the proposed technique and the existing techniques in Fig. 9 was statistically validated by the test.

The test is carried out to determine whether the differences in precision values are originated from a population with zero mean:

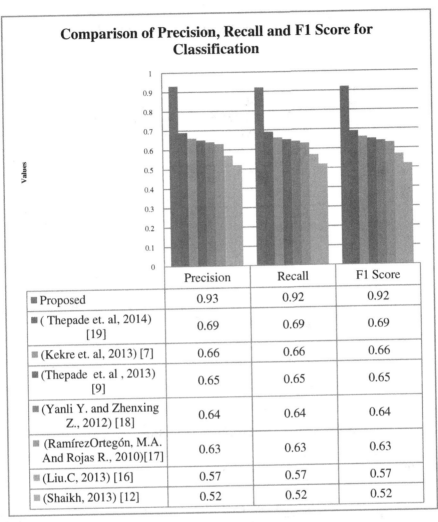

Fig. 9. Precision recall and F1 score of classification with various techniques

$$H0 : \mu d = 0 \text{ vs. } H1: \mu d < 0$$

The *p* values in Table 1 have determined the effectiveness of evidence against null hypothesis. The *p* values have indicated significant difference in precision results for the proposed technique with respect to the existing techniques. Hence the null hypothesis was rejected and the noteworthy improvement for content based image classification with the proposed technique was established.

Hereafter, retrieval process was initiated with classified query. Precision and Recall were considered as evaluation metric for retrieval and has been given by Eqs. 10 and 11.

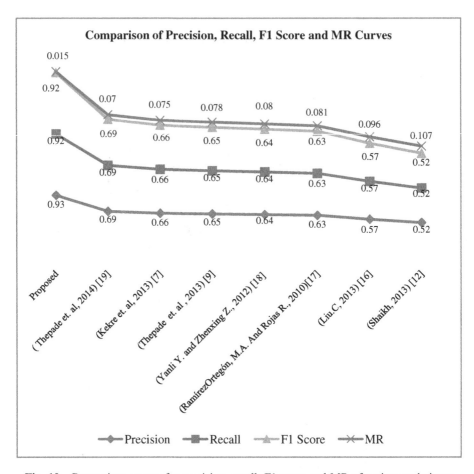

Fig. 10. Comparison curves for precision, recall, F1 score and MR of various techniques

$$Precision = \frac{Total..Number..of..Relevant..Images..Retrieved}{Total..Number..of..Retrieved..Images} \quad (17)$$

$$Recall = \frac{Total..Number..of..Relevant..Images..Retrieved}{Total..Number..of..Images..in..the..Relevant..Class} \quad (18)$$

The process of retrieval was carried out with Wang dataset. Random selection of 50 images has been performed which comprised of 5 arbitrary images from each category. At the beginning, the classification of the query image is done by fusion based distance measure using Z score normalization. Further, the classified query is used to retrieve images by searching only within the class of interest instead of searching the complete dataset as in the case for a generic query without classification. In both the cases of classified and generic query for retrieval, the retrieved images are ranked using Canberra Distance measure. Ranking process is followed by retrieval of top 20 images.

Table 1. *t test* for statistical significance in precision value for classification

Comparison	p-value	Significance of difference in precision value for classification
Feature extraction by binarization using bit plane slicing with Niblack's local threshold method (Thepade et al. 2014)	0.007	*Significant*
Feature extraction by binarization with multilevel mean threshold (Kekre et al. 2013)	0.0074	*Significant*
Feature extraction by binarization of original + even image with mean threshold (Thepade et al. 2013)	0.0079	*Significant*
Traditional feature extraction by binarization with Bernsen's local threshold method (Yanli and Zhenxing 2012)	0.0043	*Significant*
Traditional feature extraction by binarization with Sauvola's local threshold method (Ramírez-Ortegón and Rojas 2010)	0.0016	*Significant*
Traditional feature extraction by binarization with Niblack's local threshold method (Liu 2013)	0.0029	*Significant*
Traditional feature extraction by binarization with Otsu's global threshold method (Shaikh 2013)	0.0029	*Significant*

The comparison of precision and recall for retrieval with generic query and classified query has been illustrated with a sample query image in Fig. 11.

Firstly, it was applied on Corel 5 K dataset and the retrieval with classified query is observed to be 91% which is much higher than the precision of 63.5% recorded on the same dataset in [42]. In Fig. 11, the results for retrieval with generic query have yielded 17 images from the desired category named gothic Structure and 3 images from different categories namely Buses, Elephants and Mountains for Wang dataset. On the other hand, the results for classified query have retrieved all the 20 images from the category of interest which is Gothic structure.

It is observed that average precision and recall values for retrieval with classified query have surpassed the results for generic query as in Fig. 12.

Finally, the proposed technique of retrieval is contrasted to the state-of-the art techniques in Fig. 13.

Comparison shown in Fig. 13 has clearly revealed the superiority of the proposed technique over the existing techniques. Hence, it is inferred that the proposed method of retrieval has efficiently boosted up the precision and recall value compared to the state-of-the art techniques.

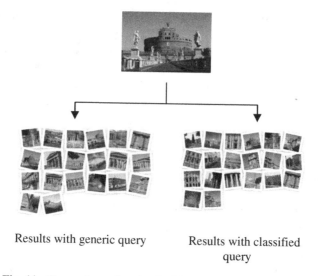

Results with generic query   Results with classified
                                           query

Fig. 11. Comparison of retrieval with generic and classified query

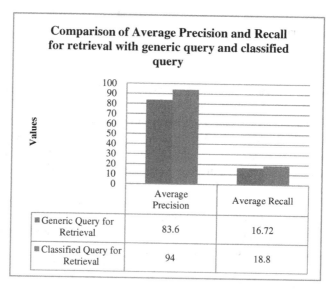

Fig. 12. Comparison of average precision and average recall for retrieval with generic and classified query

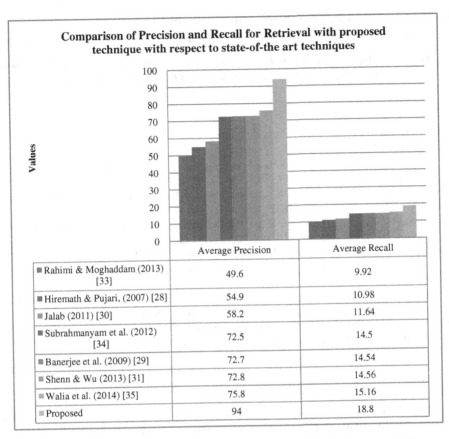

Fig. 13. Comparison of average precision and average recall with diverse techniques

7 Conclusions

The paper has carried out in depth analysis of different feature extraction techniques for content based image classification and retrieval. In this context, the authors have proposed two different techniques of feature extraction based on image binarization and Vector Quantization. The identification decisions of the two different techniques are combined for fusion based image classification. The precision, recall and F1 Score of classification with the proposed technique have surpassed the existing techniques and the precision value for classification has divulged statistical significance of improved performance. Further, the classified image is used as a query for content based retrieval. The precision and recall values for retrieval have exceeded the state-of-the art techniques and have significantly contributed to the improvement of the retrieval process. Therefore, the research work has fulfilled the following objectives:

- It has reduced the dimension of feature vectors
- It has successfully implemented fusion based method of content based image identification

- The research results have shown statistical significance
- The research results have outperformed the results of state-of-the art techniques

The work may be extended towards content based image recognition in the field of military, media, medical science, journalism, e commerce and many more.

References

1. Bashir, M.B., et al.: Content-based information retrieval techniques based on grid computing: a review. IETE Techn. Rev. **30**(3), 223–232 (2013)
2. Liao, B., Xu, J., Lv, J., Zhou, S.: An image retrieval method for binary images based on DBM and softmax classifier. IETE Techn. Rev. **32**(4), 294–303 (2015)
3. Aouat, S., Larabi, S.: Outline shape retrieval using textual descriptors and geometric features. Int. J. Inf. Retr. Res. (IJIRR) **2**(4), 60–81 (2012). doi:10.4018/ijirr.2012100105
4. Keyvanpour, M.R., Charkari, N.M.A.: Content based model for image categorization. In: 20th International Workshop on Database and Expert Systems Application, p. 4. IEEE (2009)
5. Walia, E., Pal, A.: Fusion framework for effective color image retrieval. J. Vis. Commun. Image R. **25**(6), 1335–1348 (2014). doi:10.1016/j.jvcir.2014.05.005
6. Yıldız, O.T., Aslan, O., Alpaydın, E.: Multivariate Statistical Tests for Comparing Classification Algorithms. In: Coello, C.A.C. (ed.) LION 2011. LNCS, vol. 6683, pp. 1–15. Springer, Heidelberg (2011)
7. Kekre, H.B., Thepade, S., Das, R.K.K., Ghosh, S.: Performance boost of block truncation coding based image classification using bit plane slicing. Int. J. Comput. Appl. **47**(15), 45–48 (2012). ISSN: 0975-8887
8. Thepade, S., Das, R., Ghosh, S.: Performance comparison of feature vector extraction techniques in RGB color space using block truncation coding or content based image classification with discrete classifiers. In: Annual IEEE India Conference (INDICON), pp. 1–6 (2013). doi:10.1109/INDCON.2013.6726053
9. Thepade, S.D., Das, R.K.K., Ghosh, S.: Image classification using advanced block truncation coding with ternary image maps. In: Unnikrishnan, S., Surve, S., Bhoir, D. (eds.) Advances in Computing, Communication, and Control. Communications in Computer and Information Science. Communications in Computer and Information Science, vol. 361, pp. 500–509. Springer, Heidelberg (2013)
10. Kekre, H.B., Thepade, S., Das, R., Ghosh, S.: Multilevel block truncation coding with diverse colour spaces for image classification. In: IEEE-International Conference on Advances in Technology and Engineering (ICATE 2013), pp. 1–7 (2013)
11. Otsu, N.: A threshold selection method from gray-level histogram. IEEE Trans. Syst. Man. Cybern. **9**, 62–66 (1979)
12. Shaikh, S.H., Maiti, A.K., Chaki, N.: A new image binarization method using iterative partitioning. Mach. Vis. Appl. **24**(2), 337–350 (2013)
13. Niblack, W.: An Introduction to Digital Image Processing, pp. 115–116. Prentice Hall, Eaglewood Cliffs (1998)
14. Sauvola, J., Pietikainen, M.: Adaptive document image binarization. Pattern Recogn. **33**(2), 225–236 (2000)
15. Bernsen, J.: Dynamic thresholding of gray level images. In: Proceedings of the International Conference on Pattern recognition (ICPR 1986), pp. 1251–1255 (1986)

16. Liu, C.: A new finger vein feature extraction algorithm. In: IEEE 6th International Congress on Image and Signal Processing (CISP), vol. 1, pp. 395–399 (2013)

17. Ramírez-Ortegón, M.A., Rojas, R.: Unsupervised evaluation methods based on local gray-intensity variances for binarization of historical documents. In: IEEE 20th International Conference on Pattern Recognition (ICPR), pp. 2029–2032 (2010)

18. Yanli, Y., Zhenxing, Z.: A novel local threshold binarization method for QR image, In: IET International Conference on Automatic Control and Artificial Intelligence, pp. 224–227 (2012)

19. Thepade, S., Das, R., Ghosh, S.: A novel feature extraction technique using binarization of bit planes for content based image classification. J. Eng. 13 (2014). doi:10.1155/2014/439218. Article ID 439218. Hindawi Publishing Corporation

20. Kekre, H.B., Sarode, T.K., Raul, B.C.: Color image segmentation using Kekre's fast codebook generation algorithm based on energy ordering concept. In: Proceedings of the International Conference on Advances in Computing, Communication and Control, pp. 357–362 (2009)

21. Lai, J.Z.C., Liaw, Y.C., Liu, J.: A fast VQ codebook generation algorithm using codeword displacement. Pattern Recogn. **41**(1), 315–319 (2008)

22. Liaw, Y.C., Lo, W., Lai, J.Z.C.: Image restoration of compressed image using classified vector quantization. Pattern Recogn. **35**(2), 329–340 (2002)

23. Nasrabadi, N.M., King, R.A.: Image coding using vector quantization: a review. IEEE Trans. Commun. **36**(8), 957–971 (1998)

24. Foster, J., Gray, R.M., Dunham, M.O.: Finite state vector quantization for waveform coding. IEEE Trans. Inf. Theory **31**(3), 348–359 (1985)

25. Kim, T.: Side match and overlap match vector quantizers for images. IEEE Trans. Image Process. **1**(2), 170–185 (1992). A Publication of the IEEE Signal Processing Society

26. Lai, J.Z.C., Liaw, Y.C., Lo, W.: Artifact reduction of JPEG coded images using mean-removed classified vector quantization. Signal Process. **82**(10), 1375–1388 (2002)

27. ElAlami, M.E.: A novel image retrieval model based on the most relevant features. Knowl. Based Syst. **24**, 23–32 (2011)

28. Hiremath, P.S., Pujari, J.: Content based image retrieval using color, texture and shape features. In: 15th International Conference on Advanced Computing and Communications ADCOM, vol. 9, no. 2, pp. 780–784. IEEE (2007)

29. Banerjee, M., Kundu, M.K., Maji, P.: Content-based image retrieval using visually significant point features. Fuzzy Sets Syst. **160**(23), 3323–3341 (2009)

30. Jalab, H.A.: Image retrieval system based on color layout descriptor and Gabor filters. In: 2011 IEEE Conference on Open Systems, pp. 32–36. IEEE (2011)

31. Shen, G.L., Wu, X.J.: Content based image retrieval by combining color texture and CENTRIST. In: IEEE International Workshop on Signal Processing, vol. 1, pp. 1–4 (2013)

32. Irtaza, A. Jaffar, M.A. Aleisa, E., Choi, T.S.: Embedding neural networks for semantic association in content based image retrieval. Multimed. Tool Appl. **72**(2), 1911–1931 (2014)

33. Rahimi, M., Moghaddam, M.E.: A content based image retrieval system based on color ton distributed descriptors. Sig. Image Video Process. **9**(3), 691–704 (2015)

34. Subrahmanyam, M., Maheshwari, R.P., Balasubramanian, R.: Expert system design using wavelet and color vocabulary trees for image retrieval. Expert Syst. Appl. **39**(5), 5104–5114 (2012)

35. Walia, E., Vesal, S., Pal, A.: An Effective and Fast Hybrid Framework for Color Image Retrieval, Sensing and Imaging. Springer, New York (2014)

36. Sridhar, S.: Image Features Representation and Description Digital Image Processing, pp. 483–486. India Oxford University Press, New Delhi (2011)

37. Dunham, M.H.: Data Mining Introductory and Advanced Topics, p. 127. Pearson Education, Upper Saddle River (2009)
38. Wang, J.Z., Li, J., Wiederhold, G.: SIMPLIcity: semantics-sensitive integrated matching for picture libraries. IEEE Trans. Pattern Anal. Mach. Intell. **23**(9), 947–963 (2001)
39. Thepade, S., Das, R., Ghosh, S.: Feature extraction with ordered mean values for content based image classification. Adv. Comput. Eng. (2014). doi:10.1155/2014/454876. Article ID 454876
40. Liu, G.-H., Yang, J.-Y.: Content-based Image retrieval using color difference histogram. Pattern Recogn. **46**(1), 188–198 (2013)
41. Linde, Y., Buzo, A., Gray, R.: An algorithm for vector quantizer design. IEEE Trans. Commun. **28**(1), 84–95 (1980)
42. Zhang, S., et al.: Query specific rank fusion for image retrieval. IEEE Trans. Pattern Anal. Mach. Intell. **37**(4), 803–815 (2015)
43. Bhattacharya, P., Gavrilova, M.: DT-RANSAC: a delaunay triangulation based scheme for improved RANSAC feature matching. In: Gavrilova, M.L., Tan, C.J.K., Kalantari, B. (eds.) Transactions on Computational Science XX. LNCS, vol. 8110, pp. 5–21. Springer, Heidelberg (2013). doi:10.1007/978-3-642-41905-8_2

Author Index

Printed in the United States
By Bookmasters